THE
NEW TESTAMENT BASIS OF PACIFISM

THE
NEW TESTAMENT
BASIS OF PACIFISM

BY

G. H. C. MACGREGOR, D.Litt., D.D.

*Professor of Divinity and Biblical Criticism
in the University of Glasgow*

THE FELLOWSHIP OF RECONCILIATION
2929 BROADWAY   NEW YORK CITY

First published December 1936
Second impression April 1938
Third impression April 1940
Fourth impression June 1941
Fifth impression January 1942
Sixth impression August 1947

Price 50 cents

PHOTO-OFFSET IN U. S. A.
BY PERMISSION OF BRITISH PUBLISHERS,
JAMES CLARK & COMPANY, LONDON, ENGLAND

CONTENTS

CONTENTS

PREFACE

THIS is not a book on the practical issues involved in the problem of Peace and War. It is possible to-day to advocate Pacifism on any number of grounds; for all sensible people now realize that modern war on a large scale has become a weapon far more dangerous than any of the evils from which it is supposed to defend us. But for the Christian war is primarily a moral problem, and every moral problem is ultimately theological. For this reason it is greatly to be desired that an adequate study might be made of the theological basis of Pacifism. It is not the aim of the present volume to do this, though the fringe of the subject is touched in Chapters V and VI. Much less is it our main object to argue why and how Christian Pacifism might well prove to be practical politics in the present situation. All these problems can be intelligently discussed from the Christian standpoint only when we have first asked, What, as a matter of fact, does Jesus Himself teach? What is the bearing of New Testament doctrine as a whole on this particular question of war? Pacifists are perhaps too apt to assume without sufficient proof that Jesus' ethic is incontestably "pacifist", and that, even if so proved, He intended that pacifist ethic to be applied to the wider sphere of social and national politics. Our opponents still more light-heartedly deny this, with an even greater lack of demonstration. This little book is offered in the hope that it will provide all

Christians who are sincere workers for peace—
whether they be "Pacifists" or not—with the
material necessary for thinking through for themselves this greatest of all modern ethical problems.

G. H. C. MACGREGOR.

Glasgow,
   September, 1936.

I

THE PROBLEM: THE CHURCH AND WAR

IT is greatly to be desired that some other word than "Pacifism" might be discovered to describe the faith which includes among the first principles of its creed the total renunciation of war. In the popular mind "Pacifism" is equivalent to "passivism", and the consequences of not resorting to war are readily made to appear intolerable, because it is habitually assumed that the only alternative to going to war is *doing nothing*. But, whatever be true of other brands of Pacifism, that is not the *Christian* Pacifist position. For the Christian Pacifist the *negative* prohibition, which he conceives to rest upon war, has its source in the *positive* imperative of the Christian ethic, which commands that every valid means must be used to set wrongs right and build human relations on a new foundation, and yet forbids the use of such means as will by their very nature stultify the end in view. It follows that the Christian Pacifist position must be based, (a) *not* on the repudiation of all use of force in the dealings of man with man either as individuals or as units in the community; yet it is almost universally assumed that such a repudiation *is* the Pacifist position, and once the absurdity of that position is proved—often an easy enough task—the question is considered settled. *Nor* (b) is our position based on a literalistic interpretation of either the Sixth Commandment or certain sayings of Jesus in the Sermon on the Mount, though due weight must, of course, be given to those sayings in the context of Jesus' whole teaching. Even the Devil can quote Scripture, and to cite isolated passages wrested from their context is to use a boomerang which is apt to recoil on the head of the user. Rather must our position be based (c) on certain essential *basic principles* of the Christian ethic as set forth in Jesus' teaching and illustrated by His example. What these principles are is the question now at issue. But, subject to confirmation by our study, the following postulates may be provisionally stated for an adequate treatment of our subject.

(1) The first principle of Jesus' ethic is love towards one's neighbour.[1]

(2) This ethic is in turn based upon belief in a Father God Who loves all men impartially and sets an infinite value on every individual human soul.[2]

(3) All the teaching of Jesus must be interpreted in the light of His own way of life, and above all of the Cross by which His teaching was sealed.

The issue before us is therefore best framed, not by asking, Does the New Testament ethic ever allow the use of force in the resisting and conquering of evil? So to pose the question is to invite that unfortunate confusion of "Pacifism" with "passivism". We shall rather ask, What is the specifically Christian way of meeting and overcoming evil, as set forth in the teaching, example and Cross of Jesus Christ? Can War under any circumstances be held to be consistent with that way? When the question is thus stated, and our three postulates are kept in view, it becomes evident that, in order to find a place for war within the New Testament ethic, it is not enough to prove that Jesus recognizes the place of law in an ordered society, that He permits a moral use of force to uphold justice, that He might even allow the use of a "sword" in self-defence against

---

[1] In the broad sense in which Jesus uses the word in, e.g. Luke x. 29 ff. Matt. vii. 12 further defines this principle.

[2] Matt. v. 45; x. 29–31; xvi. 26.

bandits. This may all be true; and yet war, as we have come to know it, may so violate Jesus' essential principles, and so stultify the specifically Christian method of meeting evil, that its one certain issue will be not justice but moral and spiritual death. In a word, the Christian Pacifist position must rest in the main on a discrimination, in the light of the teaching and example of Jesus, between moral and non-moral uses of force, and on the affirmation that when called to the bar of the New Testament ethic, whatever may be said of certain other exercises of force, war at least is seen to be under a final prohibition.

It should be hardly necessary to insist that, inasmuch as our problem is one not of political expediency but of moral obligation, the final court of appeal is the New Testament. Yet, as concerns this particular problem, the average Christian is still in such bondage to the traditional dogma of Church and State, so painfully evolved by orthodox Protestant theology,[1] that one feels a good deal of sympathy with the outburst of G. J. Heering: "If the pure and exalted ethic of the Gospel is to come into its rights, it will have to hold dogmatics at arm's length for the present, to prevent the latter from paralysing it before it has been able to display its power and aim."[2] The aim of the following pages is to allow the authentic accents of the New Testament to be heard.

One would have hoped that, whatever our difference of opinion as to the validity and practicability under modern conditions of Jesus' teaching, it would at least be possible to reach agreement as to what the teaching actually is, even in its bearing upon so complex a problem as that of Peace and War. Yet the most sincere Christians still find

[1] For this see Chapter VII.
[2] G. J. Heering, *The Fall of Christianity*, p. 10.

themselves poles apart in their interpretation of the evidence. Few will deny that war *as an instrument of national policy* (the qualification is often important) is a complete denial of the teaching, spirit and methods of 'Jesus. But there agreement ends, and generally speaking Christians may be grouped according as they hold one of three views.

(1) Firstly it is urged that the teaching and example of Jesus are essentially "pacifist" and reveal, above all in the Cross, an alternative method of meeting and overcoming evil which renders all violent methods obsolete. War as we know it to-day, involving as it does an utter prostitution both of moral values and of the Christian conception of personal relationships, cannot under any conditions be brought within the orbit of the Christian ethic. The Church, if she is to be true to her function as the Body of Christ and His organ in society, is under all circumstances bound by that ethic, however impracticable it may appear when judged by considerations of prudence, expediency and probable result: "The foolishness of God is wiser than men; and the weakness of God is stronger than men."[1] This is the Christian Pacifist position and admits of no ambiguity.

(2) Many equally sincere Christians, among them, it must be admitted, not a few eminent dogmatic theologians, argue on the contrary that the teaching of Jesus is *not* necessarily "pacifist". Pacifism indeed appears as a dangerous modern "heresy". The New Testament ethic is based on the law of righteousness as well as on the law of love, and the besetting sin of Pacifism is to exalt love at the expense of righteousness. The Law is the basis of the Gospel, and even in the New Testament it remains not merely as so much scaffolding, to be scrapped (as is done, it is alleged by the Pacifist)

[1] I Cor. i. 25.

when its purpose is served, but as an integral part of the completed building. There are elements in both the teaching and the example of Jesus which suggest that He would approve the violent application of force in restraint of evil, and once this is admitted the line cannot be drawn even at war. The Pacifist's absolute prohibition of war rests upon a basis which is sentimental rather than ethical, and can find no support in the New Testament, which nowhere forbids the taking up of arms in a just cause. In all of which there is much truth, of which the Pacifist does well to be reminded. But is the scope of Law adequately delimited, or its final sublimation and "fulfilment" in the Gospel sufficiently · realized? These particular questions will be fully dealt with in Chapter VI.

(3) It is possible, finally, to take a middle position: Jesus' teaching, if taken at its face value and consistently applied, with due weight given to that which is distinctively His own in His method of dealing with evil, undeniably implies what to-day would be called the "pacifist" attitude. But Jesus' ethical teaching, as we have it briefly reported in the Gospels, cannot be held to cover the whole field of moral obligation with which mankind is confronted to-day. Conditions have arisen in State and Society which were not then before the mind of Jesus, who was legislating for an ideal "kingdom", and not for the imperfect world in which we live. In such a world situations are bound to arise in which the use of the war method is the lesser of two evils, even if it conflicts with Jesus' method. The Christian's duty as a citizen justifies him in refusing to take literally an ethic which he might feel constrained to obey if the Kingdom of Heaven had come on earth. According to this third point of view the debate should not be concerning any ambiguity in Jesus' teaching, which is admitted to be unequivocally

pacifist, but rather concerning its comprehensiveness, its practicability, the point at which for the Church it becomes fully applicable in our slow progress towards a completely Christian social and inter-national order. The ethic of the Sermon on the Mount must be acknowledged to be unambiguous: but meantime circumstances compel us to declare a "moratorium" upon it.

It is perhaps not entirely without significance that, over against the purely dogmatic theologians, with their possibly exaggerated deference to traditional Church dogma, this is the position adopted by several eminent New Testament scholars who are not themselves Pacifists. Professor H. Windisch, one of the foremost modern continental New Testament scholars, will serve as an example: "Condemnation of all forms of war is the only attitude congenial with the spirit of the Sermon on the Mount."[1] "The critic must concede to the objector to military service that his exegesis is the more accurate. He cannot defend himself against Tolstoyan practice by any dogmatic exegesis."[2] Windisch further quotes with full approval the opinion of Professor Baum-garten, which is all the more impressive as both are non-Pacifists writing during the Great War: "Not only the war of aggression but also defensive warfare is ruled out by the Sermon on the Mount. . . . We have primarily to recognize, however hard it may be at present (1915) to do so, that the waging of war has no place in the moral and spiritual teaching of Jesus."[3] But this ethic of Jesus, unambiguously pacifist as it is, may not be applic-able to all modern circumstances: "The Gospel con-demned the military calling. But in the face of the Gospel we must recognize the fact that the Gospel

---

[1] *Der Sinn der Bergpredigt*, 1929, p. 150.
[2] *Theol. Rundschau*, 1915, p. 288.
[3] Ibid., pp. 338, 348.

only imperfectly noted the development of 'this world'. . . . This deflection of world-history from the hopes Jesus had has brought about contingencies in no way provided for by the Gospel." This development of history "has brought to light moral laws for which no sanction can be found in the Gospel". "Jesus has nothing to do with force, army or war, but only a part of our morality is rooted in the Gospel."[1] Similarly Harnack: "It requires no further proof to establish firmly that the Gospel excludes all violence, and has nothing in common with war, nor will permit it."[2] Yet Harnack vigorously defends participation in war by Christians! In a word, the view of such scholars is that the ethic of Jesus is indisputably pacifist, but it is not comprehensive enough to be applicable to the affairs of the modern state and nation. While acknowledging the scientific honesty of such a position, which is greatly to be preferred to that of the apologist who seeks to discover loopholes through which war may actually be brought within the pale of Christian ethics, we shall have to ask whether such a compromise either does justice to the New Testament imperative, or can permanently satisfy the enlightened Christian conscience.

[1] *Theol. Rundschau*, 1915, p. 349.
[2] *Militia Christi*, p. 2. I am indebted for these quotations to G. J. Heering, *The Fall of Christianity*, pp. 31, 35, 63, 64.

II

DOES THE NEW TESTAMENT SANCTION WAR?

BOTH sides to the present controversy must plead guilty to the unfortunate practice of quoting isolated texts, often wrested from their context; and in view of the constant and light-hearted misapplication of certain well-known passages, it will be well to deal with them, before entering upon a more positive and constructive study of the New Testament evidence. The passages will first be quoted from the Revised Version; the use made of them by certain apologists for militarism will then be indicated, and, where necessary, a corrective will be provided. We shall confine ourselves to the New Testament. Admittedly much use is made in certain quarters of passages drawn from the more war-like sections of the Old Testament, and statements such as the following are still surprisingly common: "From this verse (Matt. v. 39) has been drawn the doctrine of non-resistance. As applied to war this means that Christians are never to fight. . . . Now we have to ask, How does this doctrine harmonize with other parts of Holy Scripture? . . . And when that question is asked, we observe that the doctrine of non-resistance in war directly contradicts the plain teaching of the Old Testament. . . . When we remember how clearly military service is shown, in the Old Testament, sometimes to be according to the mind of God, we have simply to set aside the pacifist doctrine of non-resistance as applied to war."[1] Now

[1] Isaac Jolly, *Pacifism at the Bar of Holy Scripture and History*, pp. 15–17.

the question whether the will and the hand of God are to be traced in the aggressive wars of Israel is one that must be frankly faced.[1] But our present task is not the philosophy of history but the interpretation of Scripture, and if the New Testament is always to be understood in the light of the Old, rather than the Old Testament re-interpreted in the light of the New, then we may well despair of any progress towards the truth. "For the man who relates the question of Christianity and War to the whole Bible, while regarding the Bible as a unity, the whole of which lies on one level, the problem is insoluble. But he for whom the Scriptures are not a static unity, but an organic (for an organism passes through phases of growth), a progressive and ever fuller revelation of God's being and will, *he* will be able to see an ascending line, which finds its goal and zenith in Jesus Christ."[2] Moreover it often seems to be forgotten that Jesus prefaces the most crucial of all our passages with the words, "Ye have heard that it was said by them of old time . . . But I say unto you . . ."[3] Could Jesus have possibly indicated more clearly that He claimed, and was indeed exercising, the right to correct the misconceptions even of the Old Testament Scriptures themselves? As Windisch again well says: "The brutal dictates of War and State in the Old Testament simply do not arise for the man who has grasped the antitheses of the Sermon on the Mount."[4]

THE CLEANSING OF THE TEMPLE[5]: especially John ii. 15, " **And he made a scourge of cords, and cast all out of the temple, both the sheep and the oxen.**" Jesus, it is argued, was no pusillanimous

---

[1] This subject is touched upon in Chapter V.

[2] Heering, *The Fall of Christianity*, p. 19.

[3] Matt. v. 21, 27, 33, 38, 43.

[4] *Der Sinn der Bergpredigt*, 1929, p. 154.

[5] Mark xi. 15–18; Matt. xxi. 12–13; Luke xix. 45–6; John ii. 13–17.

B

centurion should give up the profession of arms.
Jesus, then, would give no countenance to Pacifism.
A similar use is made of Luke iii. 14 ff., where John
the Baptist answers the soldiers' questions without
condemning their calling. Thus Augustine, quoted
by Calvin with approval: "If Christian discipline
condemned all wars, when the soldiers asked counsel
as to the way of salvation, they would have been
told to cast away their arms. . . . Those whom
he orders to be contented with their pay, he certainly
does not forbid to serve."[1] In reply we may note:

(1) It was the centurion's faith, not his calling,
which Jesus commended. Moreover this is one of
the very few occasions on which Jesus is said to have
"marvelled". The chief impression left by the
story is that Jesus was greatly surprised to find faith
in so unlikely a quarter, though doubtless this was
chiefly because the man was a heathen.

(2) An "argument from silence" is always
precarious, and never more so than when applied to
the Gospels. Modern scholarship is insisting more
and more that only an exceedingly limited number
of motives has determined the selection of material
which has found a place in the earliest collections.
Even sayings of Jesus would tend to be excluded, if
they appeared irrelevant to the main end in view,
however useful they might prove to-day for the
solution of our modern problems. That end was the
proclamation of the Christian Gospel of salvation.
As Dr. Martin Dibelius says, "The first Christians
had no interest in reporting the life and passion of
Jesus objectively to mankind. . . . They

---

[1] There is a certain unconscious humour in the fact that in the
Westminster Confession, Chapter XXIII, the first New Testament
authority cited in support of the proposition that "Christians
. . . may lawfully, now under the New Testament, wage war
upon just and necessary occasions" is Luke iii. 14: "And
soldiers also asked him saying, And we, what must we do?
And he said unto them, *Do violence to no man* . . ."

Pacifist, but a man capable of righteous anger, which expressed itself in an act of aggressive personal violence against the desecrators of the Temple. What better justification does a Christian need even for aggressive warfare in a just cause?

This scene admittedly indicates a reaction against evil on the part of Jesus much more strenuous than the meek acquiescence which is commonly misrepresented as Pacifism. But we are not concerned to deny that there is room in Jesus' ethic for a discriminating use of force. Note, however, the following points:

(1) It is the Fourth Gospel alone which mentions the "scourge". Jewish tradition held that the Messiah at his coming would bear a lash for the chastisement of evil-doers. Scholars are agreed that the whole significance of the scene in this Gospel is Messianic, and the Evangelist's well-known love of symbolism suggests that the "scourge" is to be regarded as an emblem of authority rather than as a weapon of offence. But even if the word is to be taken literally, a correct rendering of the Greek makes it clear that the whip was used only on the animals.[1] Finally, the word[2] which in its English

---

[1] The Greek here is: πάντας ἐξέβαλεν ἐκ τοῦ ἱεροῦ, τά τε πρόβατα καὶ τοὺς βόας.

Note (a) a common and correct use of the particles τε . . . καὶ is to subdivide a subject or object, previously mentioned, into its component parts. Here " πάντας ", "all of them" (i.e. all the animals), is further defined as consisting of "sheep" (πρόβατα) and "oxen" (βόας). Cf. Matt. xxii. 10: πάντας οὓς εὗρον, πονηρούς τε καὶ ἀγαθούς. Another good example is Rom. ii. 9–10, where the construction occurs twice. Cf. also Luke xxii. 66.

(b) It is sometimes objected that, if πάντας referred only to the animals, it should naturally be in the neuter gender agreeing with πρόβατα (the nearest word), rather than masculine agreeing with βόας; being masculine it must refer to the men. But the grammatical rule is that, when one adjective qualifies two nouns of different genders, it will agree with the masculine or feminine noun rather than with the neuter noun, irrespective of position. A good example is Heb. iii. 6: ἐὰν τὴν παρρησίαν καὶ τὸ καύχημα τῆς ἐλπίδος μέχρι τέλους βεβαίαν κατάσχωμεν.

[2] ἐκβάλλειν

dress "cast out" gives the impression of extreme violence, is frequently used in the New Testament without any such suggestion, e.g. "Pray ye therefore the Lord of the harvest, that he *send forth* labourers into his harvest."[1] The parallel verse in Mark might quite legitimately be translated without any hint of exceptional violence: "He entered into the temple, and began to *send out* them that sold and them that bought in the temple."[2]

(2) Had Jesus used violence, He must inevitably have provoked retaliation and been overpowered by superior numbers. Much more probably it was the compelling "authority" of His words which over-awed His opponents; their conscience condemned them, and they withdrew in disorder. Moral authority, unarmed, triumphed where violence would have been futile. There would seem to be an argument here for Pacifism at least equal to that against it.

(3) In any case the passage has no relevance whatever to war. "My house", says Jesus, "shall be called a house of prayer *for all the nations*, but ye have made it a den of robbers."[3] Probably the scene of the desecration was the outer Court, which was open to Gentiles. The foreigner was being robbed of his right of approach to Israel's God. An incident which is so often adduced as an apology for war can in fact be read as a protest by Jesus on behalf of international goodwill.

THE CENTURION AT CAPERNAUM[4]: "**Jesus marvelled and said to them that followed, Verily I say unto you, I have not found so great faith, no, not in Israel.**" It is pointed out that Jesus commends the centurion, and never hints that there is anything wrong in the occupation of a soldier, or that the

[1] Matt. ix. 38.
[2] Mark xi. 15.
[3] Mark xi. 17.
[4] Matt. viii. 5–10; Luke vii. 1–10.

wanted nothing else than to win as many as possible to salvation in the last hour just before the end of the world, which they believed to be at hand. This salvation had been revealed in Jesus, and any morsel of information about Jesus was full of meaning for them *only when it pertained to salvation*." "The aim of the Gospels is to furnish proof of the message of salvation which has been preached."[1] Moreover, the story of the centurion belongs to a group of what have been called "Pronouncement Stories", whose "chief characteristic . . . is that they culminate in a saying of Jesus which expresses some ethical or religious precept".[2] In other words the interest of such stories is focused upon one particular motif, in this case upon the centurion's faith and Jesus' response to it. We have no right, therefore, to expect to find in it an estimate by Jesus, either favourable or otherwise, of the supplicant's military calling, nor to deduce anything from His silence. In the same chapter in Luke[3] Jesus commends "a woman in the city, which was a sinner", but He is not supposed to condone her prostitution because He is silent about it. He commends Zacchaeus the tax-collector[4] without referring to his profession: must He be held therefore to condone "graft"? The New Testament contains no word of protest against slavery: are we to conclude, therefore, that slavery is in accordance with the Christian ethic, and that those who led the protest against it were perverting the Gospel?

(3) The question of war hardly arises here. The Roman soldiery in Palestine corresponded rather to a police-force; and Jesus could not have publicly condemned such service, even had He desired to do

---

[1] *Gospel Criticism and Christology*, 1935, pp. 16, 31. Italics mine.

[2] See Vincent Taylor, *The Formation of the Gospel Tradition*, pp. 63 ff.

[3] Luke vii. 36 ff.   [4] Luke xix. 9.

so, without coming into premature conflict with Rome, and ultimately identifying Himself with violent revolt, to the stultification of His own pacifist ethic. There is much about which both Jesus and the early Church were silent because of their eager expectation of the "Kingdom's" imminent coming, which would render obsolete any denunciation of Rome and her ways.

(4) It should surely be obvious that one may gladly recognize splendid qualities in individual soldiers, as in all other professions, without thereby committing oneself to approval of their calling. It is interesting to find the militaristically minded, but honest, Harnack writing thus of the three centurions in the Gospels: "These stories are not told with a view to glorifying the soldier's profession. . . . In all these cases it is of secondary importance to the narrative that the men were soldiers. It is very true that these stories have since been exploited again and again in the interest of the profession of war."[1] And Windisch concludes a reference to our passage by remarking: "Here again the attitude of Jesus gives no sanction to militarism."[2]

" Think not that I came to send peace on earth : I came not to send peace, but a sword."[3] It is often argued from this saying that Jesus foresaw the inevitability of war under the Christian dispensation, and indeed conceived that the purpose of His mission would find its fulfilment in war rather than in peace. It is part of the presumption of Pacifism to assume that the Kingdom must be one of universal peace. But:

(1) Does this verse really express *purpose*? More probably it is a good example of a common Semitic

---

[1] *Militia Christi*, p. 52.
[2] *Theol. Rundschau*, 1915, p. 343.
[3] Matt. x. 34; cf. Luke xii. 51.

idiom whereby what is really a consequence, especially a tragic one, is ironically expressed as a purpose.[1] Jesus means, "I came on a mission of mercy, and the only result, alas, is a 'sword.'"

(2) As a matter of fact there is no reference whatever in the verse to war. Are we seriously to picture the daughter using the "sword" upon her mother? Instead of "sword" Luke here much more literally has "*division*" (διαμερισμός), the same word as in Hebrews iv. 12: "The word of God is living, and active, and sharper than any two-edged sword, and piercing even to the *dividing* of soul and spirit." Just as the word of God is said to sift the component parts of a man's being, so will Jesus' mission sift the true from the false in human society. The context shows that the "division" in question has nothing to do with war, but refers to the misunderstanding and even persecution to be endured by the loyal Christian at the hands of those who should be his best friends. The words might find a true illustration, not in a war supposedly sanctioned by Jesus, but far more fittingly in the conscientious objector to war, ostracized by society, disowned even by his own family, on account of loyalty to Jesus' teaching as he understands it.

" **When ye shall hear of wars and rumours of wars, be not troubled: these things must needs come to pass.**"[2] With this saying may be compared the various prophecies of war in the Apocalypse.[3] What right, it is asked, has the Christian to renounce war,

---

[1] A good example from the Old Testament is Hosea viii. 4: "Of their silver and their gold have they made them idols, that they may be cut off," i.e. "with the result that they have been cut off".

[2] Mark xiii. 7, and parallels.

[3] Rev. vi. 4-8; xi. 7 ff.; xii. 7 ff.; xiii. 7; xvi. 16; xvii. 14; xix. 11-21.

when Jesus Himself foretells that "it must needs come to pass"? "I would very much like to know", runs a typical "letter to the Editor", "what justification writers have for their extreme pacifist views. Whether we wish it or not, we still have the Battle of Armageddon to face. Will these friends then, when the great battle of Christ's forces against anti-Christ takes place, be pacifists?"[1] We may remark in reply:

(1) It is hardly necessary at this time of day to caution the intelligent reader against fantastically literal interpretations of the Book of Revelation. The saying of Jesus Himself, if such it is, requires much more careful consideration. But it is probable that here, too, we have a highly-coloured picture, characteristic of Jewish Apocalyptic, of the catastrophes which are to precede the end of the age. It is very doubtful whether Mark xiii. 7-8 can be considered as belonging to the authentic teaching of Jesus. Modern scholars are almost unanimous in regarding this chapter as a composite section consisting of a short independent Jewish, or Jewish-Christian, apocalypse, which has been combined with genuine sayings of Jesus. The Jewish stratum appears to consist of verses 7-8, 14-20, 24-7, which if read consecutively will be found to hang together to form an independent unit. It is in the intervening verses that we may expect to find genuine sayings of Jesus.

(2) The warning of a dire succession of wars has proved only too tragically true. But, even if we should feel compelled to accept this as an authentic saying of Jesus, it is not necessary to conclude that, contrary to the whole trend of His teaching, Jesus has laid upon His disciples the obligation to take part in such wars, which are due in part, as He Himself suggests, to the emergence of "false Christs

[1] *British Weekly*, August 30th, 1934.

and false prophets" who will "lead astray, if possible, even the elect."[1]

(3) As for the warlike passages in the Book of Revelation, we may allow G. J. Heering to give us a summary of his own conclusions and those of other scholars: "Christian apocalyptic was built up in the first century on the Jewish model, and largely out of Jewish materials of which the Revelation of St. John is the biblical example. Harnack writes: 'The apocalyptic eschatology preserves traces of the warlike Messiah by taking them over to its portrait of Jesus,' but 'one notices that the warlike element is wholly confined to the apocalyptic eschatology, and does not extend to the figure of Christ outside it.' And as the Messiah of apocalypse fights with angels at his side, and not with men, this action in no way affects the example which the Christ of the Gospels has left behind. 'Heavenly beings and superhuman heavenly powers alone wage war on God's behalf. When men fight, they are doomed to destruction; only the devil lets men fight for him.' The author of Apocalypse is convinced of that."[2]

"But now, he that hath a purse, let him take it, and likewise a wallet; and he that hath no sword, let him sell his cloke and buy one. For I say unto you, that this which is written must be fulfilled in me, And he was reckoned with transgressors: for that which concerneth me hath fulfilment. And they said, Lord, behold, here are two swords. And he said, It is enough."[3]

A typical comment from the anti-pacifist viewpoint is that of the German theologian Spitta during the war: "See! Jesus has summoned His followers

[1] Mark xiii. 22.
[2] Heering, *The Fall of Christianity*, p. 30, quoting Harnack, *Militia Christi*, p. 6, and Windisch, *Der Mess. Krieg*, p. 76.
[3] Luke xxii. 36–8.

to armed defence! He was no tender pacifist."[1]
Is there any reply?

(1) It must be frankly confessed that the passage
is one of the most puzzling with which we have to
deal, and it has always perplexed scholars, even
when they have no axe to grind in connection with
the present controversy. Thus Weiss writes in his
famous *Commentary*: "The martial note in this
word is in direct contradiction to many others which
definitely forbid resistance. It is in direct opposition to the whole spirit of primitive Christianity."
If Spitta's comment is justified, then it is very hard
to explain Jesus' complete change of front when His
disciples take Him at His word and put up an armed
defence in Gethsemane: "Put up again thy sword
into its place: for all they that take the sword shall
perish with the sword."[2]

(2) Short of a definitely pacifist explanation, much
the best interpretation is one suggested to me by
my colleague, Principal W. A. Curtis: "It is evident
that Jesus had not forbidden the disciples in their
journey from Galilee to Jerusalem to carry weapons,
and that these weapons were nothing but the
customary means of protection which travellers have
always used *when beyond the reach of law* and armed
protection. In Jerusalem they were *under the
shadow of the law*, Jewish and Roman, and their arms
were in abeyance. In the passage quoted the
traveller's sword is like the purse, and the wallet,
and the sandals, and the cloak, a symbol of homeless
wandering on an urgent and dangerous mission, far
more formidable than their shorter and safer errands
hitherto at His bidding. It may be inferred that
Jesus had taken no exception to them bearing the
ordinary means of self-defence when travelling in

[1] *Theol. Rundschau*, 1915, p. 235; quoted by Heering, op. cit.
p. 24.
[2] Matt. xxvi. 52.

bandit-infested country *beyond the protection of armed authority*." (Italics throughout are mine.) The point of this interpretation is the distinction drawn between Jesus' permission of arms when "beyond the reach of law", and His prohibition of them "under the shadow of the law". This is thought to explain Jesus' apparent *volte face* at the arrest. It is also assumed that Jesus envisages henceforth a more "dangerous and urgent mission", which will take the disciples to a greater extent than hitherto beyond the pale of law, and therefore justify the bearing of defensive arms. This exegesis is admittedly attractive: but there are serious difficulties:

(a) The command to "buy a sword" appears to be given with the prospect of Jesus' coming arrest and death definitely in view, and with the purpose of meeting some eventuality connected with this coming crisis: verse 37, "*For* . . . that which concerneth me hath fulfilment," makes this quite plain.

(b) Yet, if anything is certain, it is that the command cannot have been given with a view to resistance at the arrest; Jesus' rebuke, "Put up thy sword again into its place,"[1] rules this out.

(c) It is difficult, again, to see how the approach of Jesus' death, or even the Crucifixion itself, should be thought of as so altering the disciples' circumstances that, whereas formerly they travelled under the protection of common law, where no "sword" was needed, they would henceforth be travelling (as this interpretation assumes) "beyond the protection of armed authority", where possession of arms might be permitted. The interpretation seems somewhat arbitrarily to read into the passage this distinction between two environments, one "under the shadow of the law" and the other "beyond the reach of the law". The distinction is, of course, a

[1] Matt. xxvi. 52.

real one; but it is doubtful whether it is implied in this passage.

(3) Many modern scholars have accordingly suspected the passage, and even the connection of verse 36 with verse 38 is questioned. The incident occurs only in Luke, and it is perhaps suggestive that in the sequel[1] this Evangelist tones down Jesus' sharp rebuke as recorded by Matthew[2] into the ambiguous words, "Suffer ye thus far." It is not a little tempting to guess that our crux is simply an awkward attempt on the part of the "Lukan editor" to prepare the way for the sequel in Gethsemane, and so to justify the disciples' attempt at violent resistance. It is significant that elsewhere Luke tends to slur over the shortcomings of the Twelve. For example, while Mark tells frankly of the unworthy claim made by James and John to places of special honour in the Kingdom,[3] and Matthew begins the white-washing process by transferring the blame to their mother,[4] Luke tactfully omits the incident altogether.

(4) If this be considered too drastic a cutting of the knot, we are left with three alternatives. The command to "buy a sword" must be taken either:

(a) Quite literally and seriously, as the opponents of Pacifism assert. But, as J. M. Creed in the most up-to-date commentary in English on St. Luke's Gospel puts it, "It is unlikely that Jesus seriously entertained the thought of armed resistance, which indeed would be in conflict with the whole tenor of His life and teaching."[5] Similarly F. C. Burkitt: "It is impossible to believe that the command to buy a sword was meant literally or seriously."[6] It

[1] Luke xxii. 51.
[2] Matt. xxvi. 52.
[3] Mark x. 37.
[4] Matt. xx. 20.
[5] *The Gospel according to St. Luke*, p. 270.
[6] See *The Gospel History and its Transmission*, pp. 140 ff.

should perhaps be remarked that neither of these scholars is a Pacifist.

(b) Seriously, but metaphorically. "It seems better", writes Dr. Creed, "to assume that Jesus intended the words of verse 36 to be accepted in a general sense as a warning that disaster is coming,[1] and that the disciples misunderstand Him."[2] Then Jesus, in despair at the denseness of His hearers who have taken Him up literally and produced two swords, breaks off the conversation with the common Semitic formula, "It is enough!"[3]

(c) Literally, but ironically—the words being spoken by Jesus in what Dr. Burkitt calls a mood of "ironical foreboding". The words "it is enough" might then be taken as a semi-playful rejoinder to the literally-minded disciples. The absurdly inadequate "two swords" are "enough" with which to resist the might of Rome! So far from being a summons to armed defence, Jesus' words are rather a wistful reminder of the utter futility of armed resistance.

Our conclusion then is that these words have been made to carry much greater weight than is legitimate. But it must be allowed that, so far as this context goes (if it is read apart from the sequel in Gethsemane), we cannot cite Jesus as definitely discountenancing the recognized habit of carrying arms in self-defence. But, even so, is it necessary to suppose that, where a Livingstone was content to go armed only with the Gospel of love, the Master Himself and His company, in contradiction to the whole spirit and trend of His teaching, would rely upon "swords"?

"All they that take the sword shall perish with the sword."[4] This is quite commonly interpreted as

[1] Cf. Matt. x. 34; Luke xii. 51.
[2] Creed, op. cit. p. 270.
[3] See Deut. iii. 26; and cf. the similar phrase in Mark xiv. 41.
[4] Matt. xxvi. 52.

meaning that the aggressor, no doubt, is to perish; but how, if not by the "sword" of the defender? It is argued that Jesus thus sanctions defensive warfare as an instrument necessary for the accomplishment of God's just and holy purpose.

But the saying can be thus misused only when it is wrested from its context by the omission of the first clause, " **Put up again thy sword into its place!** " For it is precisely the *defensive* "sword" which is here coming under condemnation. The sword, even when used in defence, will recoil upon him who uses it. There are not two "swords" in view, the unrighteous sword of the aggressor and the righteous sword of the defender. The "perishing by the sword" is inherent in the very use of the sword, not a penalty exacted by a third party. It is true that there is an echo of this saying in the warlike Book of Revelation, where it appears to be misunderstood in much the same way as it is by our militarists: "If any man shall kill with the sword, with the sword must he be killed."[1] But the words as spoken by Jesus are regularly interpreted by early Christian writers as an absolute prohibition of military service. Here, for example, is Tertullian: "Shall it be held lawful to make an occupation of the sword, when the Lord proclaims that he who uses the sword shall perish by the sword?"

" **When the strong man armed guardeth his own court, his goods are in peace** "[2]—from which it is argued that according to Jesus Himself the only true security is to be armed to the teeth. To refute such exegesis it is only necessary to read on: " **But when a stronger than he shall come upon him, and overcome him, he taketh from him his whole armour wherein he trusted, and divideth his spoils.** " If

[1] Rev. xiii. 10.
[2] Luke xi. 21 f.

security lies in arms, then it is only when each man is stronger than all his neighbours! The whole stress is upon the futility of "the armour wherein he trusted". In any case there is no reason to suppose that Jesus blesses war merely because He uses a simile drawn from arms. Is He to be thought to bless burglary when He compares the coming of the Son of Man with the breaking in of a thief?[1]

"**If my kingdom were of this world, then would my servants fight.**"[2] Jesus is explaining that a Kingdom such as His is not one which is defended by force of arms, for "it is not of this world". Yet the inference has actually been wrung from the verse that conversely, when the issue *is* one of loyalty to a worldly kingdom, Jesus *would* have His servants fight. Even Luther argues from this passage that Jesus had no quarrel with war itself, provided it were waged by the Sovereign for just ends. Were Jesus a worldly Sovereign, He would do the same.

But the saying begins, "**My kingdom is NOT of this world.**" One might as well argue that, if Jesus' view of His mission and purpose were the opposite of what in point of fact it is, then His ethical teaching would be likely to suffer a similar metamorphosis—which is obvious, but not very helpful! The very essence of the New Testament challenge is surely that the Christian is to practise here in the world an ethic which is not of the world.

"**But the king was wroth; and he sent his armies, and destroyed those murderers, and burned their city.**"[3] Together with this verse we may consider other similar parabolic illustrations.[4]

[1] Matt. xxiv. 42 ff.
[2] John xviii. 36.
[3] Matt. xxii. 7.
[4] Cf. Matt. xviii. 34 f.; xxiv. 50 f.; xxii. 13; xxv. 30; Mark xii. 9; Luke xix. 27, etc.

It is sometimes argued that various allusions in
Jesus' parables, for example descriptions of kings and
masters inflicting severe penalties on offending
subjects, must be held to imply that Jesus would
approve a similar application of armed violence and
other forcible social sanctions to wrongdoers in real
life. A correct appreciation of the whole trend and
method of Jesus' teaching will decisively negative
any such suggestion. In His parabolic illustrations
Jesus can be held neither to approve nor condemn
the actual practices from which they are drawn.
He always uses these illustrations to underline some
one fundamental moral or spiritual truth. For
example, Luke xvii. 7-10 has as its central thought
the truth that the Christian is always on duty. It
does not teach that the Christian himself may own
and overwork slaves!

" **Put on the whole armour of God,**"[1] and numerous
other Pauline military metaphors.[2] Surely, it is
argued, Paul must approve of warfare, or else he
would not so constantly use military metaphors to
describe the Christian way of life.

Once again a study of the context is sufficient
refutation. The emphasis is regularly upon the
contrast between ordinary warfare and the Christian
way of life: " **Our wrestling is** NOT **against flesh and
blood.**"[3] The Christian will fight only with the
weapons of the Spirit. It would be truer to argue
that Paul deliberately uses the figure of military
warfare in order to stress the point that the warfare
of the Christian is something wholly different. The
Christian must discover "the moral equivalent of
war." It is " **the good fight of faith** " which is in

[1] Eph. vi. 10–17.
[2] Cf. Rom. xiii. 12; 2 Cor. vi. 7; 1 Thess. v. 8.; 1 Tim. i. 18;
vi. 12; 2 Tim. ii. 3 f.
[3] Eph. vi. 12.

question.[1] No early Christian would have dreamed of appealing to such metaphors in justification of war; the very reverse is the truth. "I am a soldier of Christ," cried a soldier-convert martyred for refusing military service, "and may not fight; the weapons of blood are discarded, that the weapons of peace may be girded on."[2]

" Greater love hath no man than this, that a man lay down his life for his friends."[3] War may sometimes be justified, so it is said, if only because it calls forth the supreme expression of this Christ-like love.

This argument must be dealt with more fully in Chapter VI. But meantime, we may remind ourselves:

(1) Jesus did *not* say, "that a man kills his enemies for the sake of his friends". Reverently though one acknowledges that multitudes have so laid down their lives in battle for the sake of their friends, so to do is not the aim and object of the soldier's training and profession. The soldier is trained to protect himself and to kill others, and the better soldier he is, the more successful will he be in doing both. The self-sacrifice is but an inevitable by-product of the soldier's main task, and we must not allow sentiment to blind us to that fact.

(2) And even higher expression of this Christ-like love is envisaged in the great words of Paul: "God commendeth His own love towards us, in that, while we were yet *sinners*, Christ died for us." Jesus died not only for His "friends". "When we were *enemies*, we were reconciled to God by the death of His Son."[4]

(3) The essence of this Christ-like sacrifice is that it should be wholly voluntary: "Therefore doth the

[1] 1 Tim. vi. 12.
[2] Quoted by Heering, *The Fall of Christianity*, p. 53.
[3] John xv. 13.
[4] Rom. v. 8, 10.

c

Father love me, because I lay down my life. . . .
No man taketh it away from me, but I lay it down of
myself."[1] Though one humbly, yet proudly, agrees
that thousands have died on the battlefield in such a
spirit, what can there possibly be in common
between such an ideal and a war-system which
conscripts free human personalities to be the
instrument of mass-slaughter and in the end to
become themselves "cannon-fodder"? We gain
nothing by mincing words.

(4) It is easy to come perilously near to
blasphemy when we thus appeal to the Cross in the
name of Mars. "The Cross", says Erasmus, "is
the banner and standard of Him who has overcome
and triumphed, not by fighting and slaying, but by
His own bitter death. With the Cross do ye deprive
of life your brother, whose life was rescued by the
Cross?"

Two other much-quoted passages should perhaps
fall to be dealt with here: Mark xii. 17, "Render
unto Caesar the things that are Caesar's, and unto
God the things that are God's"; and Romans
xiii. 1–7, where Paul writes as if he considered the
"higher powers", that is to say the "civil
authority" or the "civil magistrate", to be a
Divine institution to which loyal obedience is due.
It will be better, however, to reserve both passages
for treatment in the Chapter on "Christ and
Caesar".

[1] John x. 17 f.

III

THE WAY OF JESUS IN PERSONAL RELATIONSHIPS

WHERE are we to look for that which is specifically distinctive and original in Jesus' teaching and example concerning personal relationships, particularly with reference to the meeting and overcoming of evil? We might perhaps summarize thus: The essence of His teaching is distilled in His "Golden Rule", "All things whatsoever ye would that men should do unto you, even so do ye also unto them."[1] It is crystallized in two commandments on which He declares the whole Law to hang, complete love of God, and unfailing love of neighbour.[2] His blessing is for the peacemakers.[3] He holds it to be nearer His own spirit to suffer wrong than to inflict it, even when the suffering is undeserved.[4] Instead of seeking revenge He calls on His disciples to love their enemies and to pray for those who persecute them.[5] Not only His teaching but also His life bears witness that error must be overcome not by violence but by truth, hatred not by enmity but by love, evil not by its own weapons but by good. Finally His acceptance of the Cross was a summary in action of all that He had taught in word. And, most important of all, His ethic is founded throughout on His distinctive belief about God. The peacemakers are blessed because they are the children of

[1] Matt. vii. 12.
[2] Matt. xxii. 35–40.
[3] Matt. v. 9.
[4] Matt. v. 10–12. Note the word "falsely".
[5] Matt. v. 44.

God and share His nature.[1] His disciples will love
even their enemies, in order that they may be "sons
of their Father who is in heaven".[2] They will
strive to be "perfect", because "their heavenly
Father is perfect".[3] We have here morals founded
on theology, an ethic of the Brotherhood of Man
founded on a theology of the Fatherhood of God.

Let us follow Jesus in His application of this
ethic. It is no part of our aim to argue that this
specifically Christian ethic was intended by Jesus
either to annul the sanction of law, or to render
obsolete a civil authority capable of a moral use of
force. But it does suggest that Jesus had a profound
mistrust of all forcible methods of righting wrong,
and that He consistently urged upon His followers
a new and better way. If relationships should
become strained by some matter of personal dispute,
then every possible effort must be made towards
conciliation and agreement before appeal is made to
the common law: "Agree with thine adversary
quickly, whiles thou art with him in the way."[4]
If an individual disciple should feel himself to be
wronged by a "brother", that is by a fellow-
believer, what is he to do? His first duty is that of
forgiveness unconditional and without limit: "Peter
said to him, Lord, how oft shall my brother sin
against me, and I forgive him? until seven times?
Jesus saith unto him, I say not unto thee, Until
seven times; but, Until seventy times seven."[5]
But, though for the wronged man forgiveness is a
duty unconditional and unlimited, forgiveness can
never be complete until it wins a response in the
repentance of the wrongdoer, until the wrongdoer

[1] Matt. v. 9.
[2] Matt. v. 45.
[3] Matt. v. 48.
[4] Matt. v. 25.
[5] Matt. xviii. 21 f.

is won over and reconciliation is achieved. How is the wronged man to attain to this, in Jesus' eyes the only worth-while, "redress"? In another passage we have a hint: "If thy brother sin against thee, go, shew him his fault between thee and him alone: if he hear thee, thou hast gained thy brother. But if he hear thee not, take with thee one or two more, that at the mouth of two witnesses or three every word may be established. And if he refuse to hear thee, tell it unto the church: and if he refuse to hear the church also, let him be unto thee as the Gentile and the publican."[1] That is to say, the wronged man is not hastily to claim his right to the justice of the civil courts. Best of all, the initial act of forgiveness being assumed, he will by a personal approach remonstrate with his "brother", seek to clear away the misunderstanding, and thereby "win his brother" to his own viewpoint. Here we have the first hint of a truth to which we shall recur again and again: justice is truly vindicated, not when the wrongdoer is compelled to make reparation, but when the unjust will is "won" to justice.[2] If this best of all ways fails, the wronged man will seek a settlement by arbitration, preferably in private by one or two friends, if necessary through the mediation of the congregation of believers—but still without any recourse to the forcible sanctions of civil law. Only when all these efforts have failed is the wronged man to regard and treat the wrongdoer "as the Gentile and the publican".

Now what is the meaning of this last very puzzling injunction? For it is difficult to believe that Jesus is using the words "Gentile" and "publican" in their commonly accepted opprobrious sense. I am again indebted to Principal Curtis for a very attractive

---

[1] Matt. xviii. 15–17.
[2] This "redemptive" element in the way of Jesus will be fully discussed in Chapter VI.

suggestion: Only when all attempts at reconciliation
have failed is the wronged Christian to "invoke the
common law, which deals alike with Gentiles, tax-
gatherers, and believers. Let the law take its course
in defeat of wrong only when religious instruments
have failed. The Jew and the Christian should
settle their differences without recourse to secular
law; they have a higher standard of right. When
Jesus says, 'if he refuses to listen to the congregation
let him be unto thee as a Gentile or a tax-gatherer',
it is impossible to construe His mind in terms of an
attitude to those men which He did not countenance
or share, the ordinary Pharisaic attitude of excom-
munication or ostracism. He can only mean,
'descend to the common level of secular justice'.
This corresponds to the repeated appeal which He
makes that a Jew or a Christian will surely rise above
the level of the standards in force among the people
they have been taught to regard as below them, the
Gentiles, sinners, and publicans."[1]

If this is permissible exegesis, then the passage
may be not unfairly used to prove that Jesus did
recognize the place of law in an ordered society, and
under certain circumstances would approve appeal
to its sanctions. But it is only as a last resort, when
all the appeals of religion have been exhausted.
The passage is chiefly significant as emphasizing that
the distinctly Christian way of reacting to a
wrong against oneself is very different from the
instinctive demand of the natural man that "the
law" should protect "his rights".

So much for the disciple's treatment of a "brother"
who has wronged him. But everything which is
most truly distinctive in the ethic of Jesus comes out
most clearly when He lays down the principles which
are to govern the Christian's reaction to a wrong
against himself done not by a "brother", whom he

[1] Matt. v. 46 f.; vi. 32; Luke vi. 32 f., etc.

may be expected to love, but by an "enemy" whom he may be supposed to suspect and dislike. Even here the second of the two "great commandments"[1] is to apply: even the "enemy" is a neighbour to be loved. As Joh. Weiss well says, "This is the highest demand that can ever be made . . . the love of enemy is not just one virtue among many, but the fairest flower of all human conduct."[2] It is the "fruit" by which it shall be known whether or no Jesus' ethic is ruling a man's life.[3]

We thus arrive at what is admittedly the key-passage for our study, the "non-resistance" and "love-your-enemy" sections in Matthew v. 38-48: "Ye have heard that it was said, An eye for an eye, and a tooth for a tooth: but I say unto you, Resist not him that is evil. . . . Ye have heard that it was said, Thou shalt love thy neighbour, and hate thine enemy: but I say unto you, Love your enemies, and pray for them that persecute you; that you may be sons of your Father which is in heaven." Reserving meantime the question of the relevance of these sayings to wider social and national relationships, we shall probably be agreed that the primary reference is to the *personal* enemy, and that, however the words are to be interpreted, Jesus is here laying down, and consciously and deliberately doing so, a new principle, distinctively Christian and alternative to the commonly accepted one, which is to govern the meeting and overcoming of evil in our personal relationships. This can hardly be denied without evacuating what we have called the "antithesis of the Sermon on the Mount"[4] of all their meaning. Evil is now to be overcome, not by all those forcible

[1] Matt. xxii. 36 ff.
[2] *Commentary*, on Matt. v. 43 ff.
[3] Matt. vii. 20.
[4] Above, p. 17.

methods which are commonly slumped together
under the definition of "resistance", and by which
it is thought that an exact retributive justice, a tit
for tat, "an eye for an eye and a tooth for a tooth",
will be exacted from the wrongdoer, but by the power
of forbearing and, if necessary, suffering love. Paul
perfectly paraphrases the Master when he writes:
"Render to no man evil for evil. . . . Be not
overcome of evil, but overcome evil with good."[1]
How this new and better way caught the imagination
of the primitive Church appears from the constant
echoes of Jesus' words in the Apostolic writings.[2]

We note first that the two paragraphs, Matt. v. 38-
42 ("resist not him that is evil"), and Matt. v. 43-8
("love your enemies"), belong together as a single
whole. The apparently negative injunction to non-
resistance is immediately followed by the positive
commandment of all-embracing love. No one who
realizes this could caricature Jesus' words, as if He
meant, "Acquiesce in evil. Be passively polite to
wrongdoers. Tolerate vice. Allow the bully to rape
his victim, and stand by with folded arms while he
does so." The Pacifism of Jesus, if use the word we
must, is never "passivism". And yet "resist not
him that is evil", rightly understood, may be the
indispensable pre-requisite to "love your enemies".
There are times when a resolute refusal, merely
negative though it seems, is the only possible
foundation for an act of positive obedience, when a
"yes" to the commandment of love must be preceded
by a "no" to certain means and methods which
must inevitably render that obedience abortive. It
is only, says Jesus, when the old way has been
renounced, that the new way can be explored.

If we are willing to take these sayings at their face
value, then the way of Jesus would appear so clear

[1] Rom. xii. 17-21.
[2] See *Appendix*, p. 152 f., "Christ's Way of Meeting Evil."

that the wayfaring Christian, even though a fool, could hardly err therein. Yet this ethic—non-resistance, forbearance in the face of aggressive evil, love of enemies—is so sublime that we must all humbly confess with Heering that "only he who has believed in and experienced the redemptive love of God which Christ has revealed can truly understand and practise the Christian ethic; the two together make up the Christian life, one indivisible whole. Thus it is that the lofty and powerful claims of the Gospel ring out as self-evident truths. They are self-evident to the man who is laid hold of by God in Christ, even though—since his salvation is never finished on earth, but is always only 'in hope'—he can only live up to them in small measure, and follow Christ only from afar."[1] Yet with reference to our present problem nothing is more important than that we should ask, "What *is* the teaching of Jesus?" before we confuse the issue by going on to ask, "Is it practicable for us to-day to follow that teaching?" It will therefore be useful to glance at some of the attempts which have been made to "water down" these "self-evident truths", and thereby to "keep on good terms with the Gospel",[2] while still countenancing methods which that Gospel has made obsolete. The fact that there is a certain measure of truth in some of these attempts will perhaps help us to correct and clarify our own interpretation.

(1) It is sometimes suggested that the "exaggerated" demands of Jesus are to be explained, if not explained away, on the ground of His "eschatological" outlook, that is His supposed belief in the immediate break-up of the present world-order. The injunctions of the Sermon on the Mount may be safely "short-circuited" once it is

[1] Heering, op. cit. p. 26 f.
[2] The phrase is again Heering's, op. cit. p. 32.

realized that they are inspired by the expectation of a speedy end to the world, that they contain only an ethic for the short time between Jesus' own day and that end, an "interim-ethic" as it is called, and that therefore they are not valid for those who do not share Jesus' historical perspective.

But, quite apart from the fact that this argument, if valid, would foreclose our whole enquiry by denying that we can ever propound an ethic for to-day based on Jesus' teaching,[1] modern scholars are inclined to agree that the supposed effect of "apocalyptic" upon Jesus' moral teaching has been grossly exaggerated.[2] It may even be argued that the vivid expectation of the end of the age, so characteristic of the years immediately after Jesus, is the effect rather than the cause of these "exaggerated" demands of the New Testament ethic: a world which contemptuously rejected them was bound, Christians felt, to meet its doom.[3]

[1] "To argue that Jesus' more general principles . . . were so dependent upon the limitations of His historical outlook that they lose their validity for practical conduct as soon as those limitations are transcended, and must not be allowed to interfere with the supposed necessities of modern economics and political life, is virtually to deny that there can be any such thing as a modern Christian ethic founded on the teaching of Jesus." C. J. Cadoux, *The Early Church and the World*, p. 13.

[2] "The influence of eschatology on the ethics of the Gospel, especially on the Sermon on the Mount, is not so great as often even I myself have asserted it to be." (Windisch, *Der Sinn der Bergpredigt*, p. 152.) So also C. G. Montefiore "It is an important fact, and one of which we must take adequate note, that there is a good deal of Jesus' religious and ethical teaching which was not directly related to, or dependent upon any eschatological conceptions, any belief in the nearing end of the world . . . a good deal in His finest religious and ethical teaching which can survive such conceptions and be easily detached from them." This Jewish scholar then adds: "What is remarkable about the sayings of the Gospels is that they are often applicable to wholly alien conditions, and true even without that belief in the end of the world which underlies so many of them . . . no surer mark of their genius and first-classness." (*Synoptic Gospels*, Vol. II, p. 114.)

[3] Cf. Col. iii. 6 etc.

Moreover, it is surely significant that Jesus urges this distinctive ethic, not in view of the immediate end of the age, but, as we have seen, on the ground that it is consistent with His own conception of God's nature,[1] surely a permanent element in His teaching if anything is. In any case the "interim-ethic" theory, even if valid, could at most suggest a doubt whether Jesus' teaching is valid under modern conditions. It does not touch our present question, What *is* that teaching? Indeed, so far as the question of war is concerned, the "eschatological" argument tells in a direction quite opposite to that intended by the critics of Pacifism; for it does much to explain some of the perplexing "silences" of Jesus and the early Church concerning social and political problems.[2]

(2) It is argued, secondly, that these crucial sayings, like so much of Jesus' teaching, were spoken *ad hoc*, with reference to particular individuals in particular circumstances, and are not to be exalted into general principles binding upon all Christians. Now this is undoubtedly true of some of Jesus' most drastic demands. The command, for example, to "go, sell whatsoever thou hast, and give to the poor", is given specifically to the "Rich Young Ruler", for the special reason that in wealth Jesus saw for him the chief obstacle to discipleship.[3] But a saying with its special setting in a "Pronouncement Story"[4] is in a somewhat different category from those "timeless" sayings, without narrative framework, of which the Sermon on the Mount almost entirely consists, unless we go so far as to deny that Jesus ever laid down any general principles for universal application. It is noticeable that many

[1] Matt. v. 45, 48.
[2] See below, p. 60.
[3] Mark x. 21.
[4] See p. 21.

of His most striking and compelling sayings have
been preserved in isolation without any narrative
setting: they were felt to be so challenging, so
universally binding, that no "story" was necessary
to point the application.[1]

(3) But, it is asked again, should not these sayings
be considered as merely highly-coloured illustrations
of a general principle, in this case the principle that
"intensity" or "screwing up the standard"[2] is a
necessity in all Christian practice? Now it must
again be admitted that Jesus commonly made use of
characteristic Semitic hyperbole; and this argument
may possibly be valid in the case of an isolated and
obvious verbal hyperbole (e.g. Luke xiv. 26, "If any
man . . . *hateth* not his own father"), or when
a proposition stated literally (e.g. Matt v. 28,
"Every one that looketh on a woman to lust after
her . . .") is then pointedly illustrated by an
obvious metaphor (e.g. "If thy right eye causeth
thee to stumble, pluck it out"). But such an
explanation is surely most unlikely in the case of
teaching deliberately chosen to illustrate the
"fulfilment" of the "law" by Jesus,[3] and the
showing forth of the Divine nature in human
conduct,[4] particularly (and this cannot be too
strongly stressed) when that teaching is so entirely
and literally in line with Jesus' own way of life.
It may, of course, be freely admitted that "turning
the other cheek" is a hyperbolic Semitic illustration
of a general principle: but that principle itself is
stated, as one universally valid, in the opening words
of each paragraph, "Resist not him that is evil"

---

[1] Cf. Matt. xi. 25–30; Mark viii. 34 ff. How the general
saying about "taking the cross" is given a particular application
in a "Pronouncement Story" is seen in Mark x. 21.

[2] The phrase is Montefiore's; *Synoptic Gospels*, Vol. I, p.25

[3] Matt. v. 17.

[4] Matt. v. 45.

. . . "Love your enemies." Such considerations
seem conclusive against all such attempts to suggest
that Jesus' distinctive method of meeting evil, and
the sayings which commend it, must be understood
not literally but "spiritually" which, really amounts
to saying "*cum grano salis*". It is too often the
case that "what is stoutly called the 'spirit' of the
Sermon is rather its abrogation"; and with
reference to our present problem such methods are
only too apt to result in "war-exegesis".[1]

(4) It is suggested, finally, that we have here
"counsels of perfection" intended to apply, not to
the present world, but to the Kingdom of God which
is still to come. They are valid only in a perfect
society. Meantime we are living, not in the
Kingdom of God, but in a national state, which is a
mediating conception, a compromise if we will,
maintained by the authority of law, between the
anarchy of brute force and that régime of pure grace
which is the ultimate Christian ideal. Meanwhile
we must be content to follow the way of Jesus only
to the extent that this is possible under the conditions of human existence which God Himself has
created and still permits. Under these conditions
the ethic of the Sermon, even if it literally represents
the mind of Christ, is for the community as a whole
so impracticable as to be utterly impossible of
adoption as a practical way of life even by the
Christian Church. In other words, the Church is
justified in postponing obedience to the way of Jesus
until the coming of the Kingdom makes such
obedience so easy that it becomes "practicable" for
the whole community.

Now, apart from the fact that much of the Sermon
would be irrelevant in a perfect society, where
presumably there would be no wrongs to submit to

[1] Baumgarten, quoted by Windisch, *Theol. Rundschau*, 1915.
pp. 333, 345.

and no enemies of love,[1] this argument obscures one
of the most characteristic features of all Jesus'
teaching. Nowhere in the Gospels is it suggested
that disciples are to postpone obedience until such
obedience can be universalized. Rather are they
definitely challenged to act in the spirit of Jesus in
advance of the community. They are to go the
"extra mile"[2] along a road which the world may
call illogical, impracticable, quixotic. Otherwise
"what do ye more than others?"[3] Admittedly we
do not live in that ideal world which would make
easy the way of Christ. But, as someone has well
said, "the Christian must learn to live not as a baffled
idealist but as a rebel against the world as it is."
The Gospel of the Kingdom is not only an ideal, but
a method of attaining that Ideal. For Jesus, too,
the Kingdom was still in the future. But that did
not prevent Him from preaching a "realized
eschatology",[4] and bidding His disciples here and
now order their lives by the laws of the coming
Kingdom, promising them that if they did so the
Kingdom would break in upon them and take them
unawares.[5] As Heering caustically says, "There is
no more effective way of disabling the Gospel than
first to relegate the fulfilment of Christ's commands
to the Kingdom of God, and then to read His saying,
My Kingdom is not *of* this world, as if He had said,

[1] "It is impossible to love a person except by loving him now;
a love which proposed to operate a few years hence, or 'hereafter
in a better world than this', is plainly not love at all . . .
Whence it follows that . . . this present world comes to
have the most solemn significance as the scene where the
obligations of the Kingdom of God in a personal order are laid
upon us, and we must surrender ourselves utterly to God in their
discharge." H. H. Farmer, *The World and God*, p. 216.

[2] Matt. v. 41.

[3] Matt. v. 47.

[4] See C. H. Dodd, *The Apostolic Preaching and its Developments*,
1936, pp. 208 ff.

[5] Matt. xii. 28; Luke xi. 20.

My Kingdom is not *for* this world."[1] That the primitive Church regarded Jesus' words as injunction to be taken literally and practised here and now is perfectly clear from passage after passage.[2] Did not Jesus in His own Person set such an example?[3]

We turn therefore from Jesus' teaching to His example, for Jesus *was* what He taught, so that the best commentary upon His words is His life, just as the best interpretation of His life is His words. How then do we find Jesus in His own Person meeting and overcoming evil? Though He consistently lived by a principle of "non-resistance", yet there was nothing negative about His life. He never belittled or condoned the stark reality of evil: but He never met it with its own methods and weapons. He overcame evil with good. Nowhere, with the very doubtful exception of the Cleansing of the Temple,[4] do we find Him using force to constrain men to desist from evil or to do good; nor, with the exception of one very ambiguous passage,[5] countenancing the use of force even in self-defence. On the contrary we see Him in His own Person proving again and again that active love can win moral victories where society, with its conventional methods of coercion and penalty, was helpless. We think of the Gerasene "demoniac",[6] the woman who was a sinner,[7] the woman taken in adultery,[8] Zacchaeus,[9] the dying thief.[10] Of this aspect of Jesus' teaching the famous French scholar Loisy writes, "A country where all the honest folk conformed to these maxims would be a paradise of

---

[1] Heering, op. cit. p. 34.
[2] Cf. Rom. xii. 14 ff.; 1 Cor. iv. 12; vi. 7; 1 Thess. v. 15
1 Pet. iii. 8 f.
[3] 1 Pet. ii. 21 ff.   [7] Luke vii. 36 ff.
[4] See p. 17 f. below.   [8] John viii. 3 ff.
[5] See p. 25 f. below.   [9] Luke xix. 1 ff.
[6] Mark v. 2 ff.   [10] Luke xxiii. 39 ff.

thieves and scoundrels." He seems to have forgotten the actual effect on "thieves and scoundrels"
when Jesus Himself so dealt with them. It is
pertinent to ask whether Jesus *could* have so
succeeded, if He had *also* backed righteousness by
violent methods, if He had been ready to stone the
adulteress and only afterwards to forgive her, to
crucify the thief before He promised him Paradise.
Would the world have hailed Him as Saviour if He
had died leading the Jewish patriots against the
Roman legions instead of forgiving His enemies upon
a Roman Cross? For this positive redemptive
method of overcoming evil, when carried to the
uttermost, finds its supreme illustration in the
Cross, where Jesus refused the method of force in
dealing with the world's evil and prayed for His
enemies instead, thereby setting forth in action the
power of suffering and sacrificial love to vindicate
the moral order and recreate a sinful world.[1]

It is sometimes asked whether the verdict on
Jesus' pacifist teaching and example must not be
qualified in the light of certain violently denunciatory
sayings against, for example, the Pharisees,[2] Herod,[3]
the man who "causes little ones to stumble".[4]
Does not such denunciation show that Jesus was,
to say the least, an inconsistent Pacifist? Does it
not imply an attitude of anger and hatred which in
appropriate circumstances might result in even acts
of violence? We may take the denunciation of the
Pharisees as a test case, and perhaps the following
considerations will suffice:

[1] The bearing of the Cross on our subject is fully discussed in
Chapter VI.
[2] Matt. xxiii., especially verse 33, "Ye serpents, ye offspring
of vipers, how shall ye escape the judgement of Hell?"
[3] Luke xiii. 32, "that fox".
[4] Matt. xviii. 6, "It is profitable for him that a millstone should
be hanged about his neck, and that he should be sunk in the depth
of the sea."

(a) It is almost certain that these denunciatory sayings have been heightened by Jesus' reporters, particularly by Matthew, who is throughout his Gospel strongly anti-Pharisaic. A comparison of Matthew xxiii. with the parallel passages in Mark and Luke[1] shows that the Markan and Lukan versions are much briefer and much less "offensive". It seems clear that Matthew has sought to heighten the effect of the denunciation by adding other sayings of doubtful relevance. For example, the words in Matthew xxiii. 33, "ye serpents, ye offsprings of vipers", occur, according to Luke,[2] in an address of John the Baptist, and Matthew appears to have transferred them to Jesus.[3] Matthew, moreover, certainly records the denunciation in a vindictive spirit: "He detested the Pharisees, and gloried in the hard things Jesus had said about them."[4]

(b) There is obviously an ethical distinction between the sternest rebuke and recourse to physical violence. Yet it may be fairly objected that consistent Pacifism implies the renunciation not only of violence but of the spirit of hatred which so often prompts it. Nevertheless, righteous anger is not inconsistent with a Pacifist ethic, when it is prompted not by malice by but a love which embraces within its redemptive purpose even the object of denunciation. It is clear that Jesus' anger here had two causes: the conviction, firstly, that Pharisaic hypocrisy (i.e. the contrast between profession and practice) was one of the most serious obstacles to the

[1] Mark xii. 38–40; Luke xx. 45–7; xi. 37–52.

[2] Luke iii. 7.

[3] The metaphor is vividly apposite in Luke, where the crowds fleeing from "the wrath" are likened to snakes wriggling away from a fire in the heather. It is quite out of place when applied by Matthew to the Pharisees.

[4] See an article by W. E. Wilson in *Reconciliation*, July, 1934, p. 183.

D

effectiveness of His own message, and, secondly, that
it was leading the Pharisees themselves to destruction. The expression, "Woe unto you!" so far
from being a "curse" is expressive, not so much of
anger as of pity, and might well be translated,
"Alas for you!" The aim of Jesus' denunciation
was to turn His victims back from unreality to
truth, and so to save not only their dupes but
themselves.

(c) The denunciatory sayings must in their turn
be qualified by Jesus' express rebuke of all censorious
judgment.[1] True, the presence of these two strands
in Jesus' teaching has sometimes been made the
ground for charging Him with "inconsistency".[2]
But the fact that our own anger is in ninety-nine
cases out of a hundred tinged with censoriousness
must not blind us to the possibility that He, who was
Himself the "Truth" and the "Life", might be
moved by an anger prompted by pure love of truth
and a selfless passion to save those in peril of
spiritual death.

What, then, is our conclusion concerning the way
of Jesus in personal relationships? Though by no
definite pronouncement does He either abrogate the
function of Law in an ordered society, or explicitly
refuse to countenance under any conditions a moral
use of force, yet it is clear from both His teaching
and His example that His distinctive method of
meeting and overcoming evil rests upon presuppositions which are very different. Evil can be
truly conquered only by the power of truth and
goodness and self-sacrificing love. The moral order
can be vindicated, not by forcible restraint and
punishment of the evil-doer, but only when the will
which has defied that order is redeemed from its evil

[1] Matt. vii. 1 ff.
[2] See, e.g. the charge made by the Jewish scholar C. G.
Montefiore; Synoptic Gospels, Vol. II, p. 301.

purpose. In the light of Jesus' ethic of absolute love, of His theology of a Father God to whom every individual human soul is infinitely precious, and finally of this redemptive method of overcoming evil, it is obvious that His way will permit the use of force only within the strictest limits. Under such principles the very essence of ethical living is reverence for human personality and loving discrimination towards one's fellow-men. If under the ethic of Jesus force ever finds a proper place in personal relations, it can only be in a form which leaves ample room for this sensitive discrimination and this redemptive purpose of an all-embracing love. We are thus prepared to consider the wider application of this New Testament ethic, and its bearing upon the specific problems of war.

IV

THE WIDER APPLICATION OF THE NEW
TESTAMENT ETHIC: JESUS AND WAR

Is there any evidence that this distinctive method of meeting evil, which is so clearly laid down for His disciples in their personal relationships, was intended by Jesus to cover also a wider field of social and even national relationships? This is quite commonly denied even by Christian expositors, and the argument usually takes one of two lines.

Sometimes it is argued that Jesus propounded this ethic as a rule of life to be practised within the community of His own disciples, but that He never contemplated that it should be unconditionally practised even by Christians in their contacts with the outside world. Or, to put it otherwise, the disciple *as a disciple* is bound by the "new way", but in the ordinary daily affairs of secular life, when he is acting not in the capacity of a disciple, but in the capacity of an ordinary "man in the street", there must be many occasions when he cannot be expected to practise this way. Or again, certain forcible methods are held to have been definitely renounced by Jesus so far as they might have been used *for the advancement of His Kingdom*, which is "not of this world": but such methods might still be legitimate in His eyes, and even necessary, if practised by the rulers of a worldly kingdom. To illustrate: when Jesus said, "Whosoever would become great among you shall be your servant,"[1] the standard set up is valid only *within the Christian*

[1] Matt. xx. 26.

brotherhood, and has no relevance beyond it. Or when He repels the Devil on the Mount of Temptation,[1] He is rejecting methods which He feels to be unworthy *for the furtherance of a spiritual Kingdom* or *for the sacred end He had in view*, but He is passing no judgment on such methods when used by earthly potentates. Or when He says, "The rulers of the Gentiles lord it over them, and their great ones exercise authority over them. Not so shall it be among you,"[2] He is not in any way criticizing the kind of "authority" exemplified among the Gentiles, but is only insisting that *among His followers, in the Church*, brothers are not to exercise this kind of "authority," or "lord it" over their brethren. From this it is only a short step to argue that the words, "Put up again thy sword into its place: for all they that take the sword shall perish with the sword,"[3] imply that it is fatal to use violent methods *to advance religious ends*, but have no relevance to the use of arms in ordinary life, much less to warfare between nation and nation. In a word Jesus' distinctive ethic is framed with a view to ruling man's *religious life*, not his everyday contacts with his fellows.

Now it cannot be too strongly insisted that this "sacred-secular" distinction would have been quite meaningless to Jesus; indeed it would have been so to any good Jew of Jesus' day. For if there was one thing characteristic of contemporary Judaism it was that religion was felt to be co-extensive with life. For the Jew his peculiar doctrine of revelation implied "the bringing of all life under the control of the revealed will of God. God had a word . . . for each aspect of life however trivial. There would logically be no distinction between the sacred and

[1] Matt. iv. 8 ff.
[2] Matt. xx. 25 f.
[3] Matt. xxvi. 52.

the secular. . . . It is an anomaly to speak of
the social or the ethical implications of this religion,
because Judaism held that social and ethical as well
as 'religious' relations were explicit rather than
implicit in revelation. In its main developments
Judaism represents, accordingly, perhaps the most
thoroughgoing attempt in all history to order the
whole of life by religion."[1] Are we to think that
Jesus confined "religion" within narrower limits
than did the pious Jew of His own day? It is
inconceivable that Jesus, as a Jew, should formulate
an ethic for a "spiritual" kingdom within men's
hearts, without contemplating that its imperative
should be co-extensive with life itself.

But a much more common line of argument is that
the Gospel of Jesus, or at any rate this particular
ethic of "non-resistance" and "love of enemies",
is absolutely individualist and has no reference to the
wider relationships of the social community, least of
all to the dealings of nation with nation. To many,
perhaps most, interpreters of the Gospels it is
almost a commonplace that Jesus has no concern
whatever with the social problems and national
politics of His day. His absorbing interest lay in
the moral and spiritual life of individual men and
women. So far as He sought to redeem society He
did so exclusively by the indirect method of redeeming individual men. The idea of the "Kingdom"
in Jesus' thought had no social or national reference
whatever, but had to do with individual, inward,
and spiritual realities only. Thus the State and all
those problems which are our present study are held
to be entirely outside the orbit of His thought, and
similarly outside the scope of His ethic. This is the
conclusion, for example, of Troeltsch: "From this
point of view we can see plainly the attitude of Jesus

[1] Macgregor and Purdy, *Jew and Greek : Tutors unto Christ*,
p. 73. Cf. Moore, *Judaism*, Vol. I, p. 112, etc.

towards the State. . . . There is no thought of the State at all. Jewish nationalism and all its expectations are ignored entirely, even though Israel appears as the germ of the new world that is to be."[1] I am convinced that this is a disastrously mistaken conclusion, and that we shall never rightly evaluate the wider bearing of Jesus' ethic until we set it once again in its true historical perspective. If we are to do this, due weight must be given to the following considerations:

(1) By Jesus' contemporaries the "Kingdom of God" was undoubtedly contemplated as being the rule of God exercised over a concrete community, and was bound up with certain quite definitely national aspirations. We have no reason to suppose that John the Baptist departed in this respect from the current conception of the Kingdom, even though he warned his hearers not to presume upon their status as a chosen people.[2] Indeed the reason why John's appeal evoked such immediate response was probably because it brought to a focus the generally recognized type of expectation, though certainly with an increased moral emphasis. Jesus undoubtedly during the course of His ministry introduced into His teaching about the Kingdom new elements which enlarged and ennobled the whole conception.[3] But the Gospels make it quite clear that at the beginning of His mission He carried forward virtually unchanged the main stresses of John's message.[4] And though Jesus, too, insisted that Jewish nationality alone was no guarantee of the possession of the Kingdom, He

[1] *Social Teaching*, etc.; quoted by C. J. Cadoux in an article on "The Politics of Jesus" in *The Congregational Quarterly*, January, 1936, p. 58. This is an admirable study to which I am much indebted.

[2] Matt. iii. 9.

[3] For this see C. H. Dodd, *The Parables of the Kingdom*, especially Chapter 2.

[4] Compare Matt. iii. 1 f. with Matt. iv. 17.

still declared that it should be "given to a *nation*
bringing forth the fruits thereof".[1] Thus Jesus
seems to have accepted and worked upon the
universal assumption that the Kingdom would find
its outward expression in a theocratic national
community. Indeed, had He not done so, He must
have been largely unintelligible. Had He taken over
the idea of the Kingdom and read into it a completely other meaning, without having given clear
indication that He was so doing, He could only have
misled His hearers. Instead we find no evidence,
at any rate in the earliest records, that He sought to
disabuse His followers of the "delusion" that the
Kingdom was to find its seat in a concrete community. However "spiritual" His conception of
the Kingdom might be, His followers were still to
pray: "May thy Kingdom come, may thy will be
done, as in heaven, *so on earth*."[2] Clearly then it is
perilous to underline the purely spiritual and inward
element in Jesus' teaching to the complete elimina-
tion of the social and political elements, or to argue,
as for example does Dr. James Mackinnon, that
"Jesus was too spiritually minded to concern
Himself with the crass politics of the time. His
absorbing interest lay in the moral and spiritual
life."[3] Certainly it did: but it was in the spiritual
life of the citizens of a community renewed and
transformed because obedient to the new ethic of
the Kingdom.

(2) In line with this is the undoubted fact that
Jesus addressed His teaching in the first instance to
His own Jewish compatriots. He definitely confined
His ministry and that of His immediate circle to
Palestine.[4] His Twelve Companions are to "sit
upon twelve thrones, judging the twelve tribes of

[1] Matt. xxi. 43.   [3] *The Historic Jesus*, p. 49.
[2] Matt. vi. 10.   [4] Matt. x. 5 f.

Israel".[1] Almost regretfully, but still firmly, He insists that He "was not sent but unto the lost sheep of the house of Israel".[2] We note, too, that Jesus had the habit of contrasting His followers, not with irreligious men in general, but simply with "the Gentiles": "If ye salute your brethren only, what do ye more than others? Do not even the Gentiles the same?"[3] "In praying do not go babbling on, as the Gentiles do."[4] "Be not therefore anxious saying, What shall we eat . . .? For after all these things do the Gentiles seek."[5] "They which are accounted to rule over the Gentiles lord it over them. . . . But it is not so among you."[6] As Dr. Cadoux well says, "The only natural antithesis to the Gentiles as such is Israel as such: and I can therefore make no sense of these passages except on the assumption that Jesus addressed His appeal to the Jews *qua* Jews, in distinction (for the time being) from the Gentile world."[7] No doubt the whole spirit of Jesus' teaching was such that Paul and the Church were certainly reflecting His mind, when they stressed the universal significance of the Gospel, and its removal of all barriers between Jew and Gentile. Yet it is clear that Jesus had a plan for His own people which was integrally bound up with His idea of the Kingdom, that He must have been profoundly concerned in the social and national problems which were crucial for His people at the time, and that His ethical teaching must have been framed with those problems in view, and with a definite bearing upon them.

[1] Matt. xix. 28.

[2] Matt. xv. 24.

[3] Matt. v. 47; the word "sinners" in Luke vi. 32 ff. is clearly less original, and is in line with Luke's pro-Gentile bias.

[4] Matt. vi. 7.

[5] Matt. vi. 32.

[6] Mark x. 42 f.

[7] *The Congregational Quarterly*, January, 1936, p. 60.

(3) If one fact about Jesus is agreed upon by
moderate scholars, it is that He thought of Himself
as Messiah. Those who doubt this do so only
because Messiahship for Him clearly meant so much
more than it did to the average Jew, that the title
might seem more likely to be bestowed upon Him
by His disciples than appropriated by Himself. But
this is virtually to reject the entire historical framework of the Gospels, and thereby foreclose our whole
discussion. Now, to whatever extent Jesus may
have modified, and did modify, the conception of
Messiahship, of one feature He could not deprive it,
without evacuating it of its whole significance and
making its claim meaningless to His hearers: and
that feature was the national character of the rôle.
Now no man in Jesus' day could claim the title of
Messiah without at once being brought face to face,
by the pressure of public opinion and the eager
enquiries of tentative followers, with a national and
political problem of the first magnitude. And this
must have been so even in the case of Jesus, however
true it may be that "His absorbing interest lay in
the moral and spiritual life". This problem was the
attitude to be taken up by the pious Jew to the alien
and hated rulers of his country. And while the
whole nation, with the possible exception of the
Sadducees and the Herodians, was keenly exercised
by this problem—Zealots, Pharisees, the "quiet of
the land" alike—it is really incredible that Jesus,
as claimant to the Messiahship, could have ignored
the problem so entirely as many scholars believe,
or could have failed to suggest a solution of it, and
indicate the bearing upon it of His general ethical
principles. "It is no exaggeration to say that the
mind of Israel was in Jesus' day *obsessed* with the
political issue; and the only inference we can draw
from the fact that Jesus had a plan for the Jews to
fulfil on earth, is that *He had something to say to them*

about the political issue that obsessed them. His acknowledgment to Pilate that He held a royal office surely puts this beyond question."[1]

(4) It is just at this point that we find justification for extending the scope of Jesus' distinctive ethic to cover the actual question of war, and indeed for believing that Jesus Himself must have consciously so applied it. "The most important characteristic of His Messiahship, speaking negatively, is to be found in His refusal to wage the Messianic war."[2] And this, although leadership in such a war was precisely what all His followers would expect of Messiah. Such an overthrow of the Gentile empire by the might of God's Anointed had been foretold both by the Old Testament prophets and by the Jewish Apocalyptic writings; and however opinions differed as between Zealots, Pharisees and the "quiet of the land" as to the best way to hasten such a victory, it was universally associated with the appearance of Messiah. And in Jesus' day, to quote Cadoux once more, this expectation "was still further supported by the normal human view of tyrant empires and unwilling subjects: no one could deny that there was a good *casus belli*. Whatever, therefore, was the solution Jesus offered, it must have been fashioned in some direct relation, either positive or negative, to the prevailing expectation regarding the conquering Messiah's rôle." Yet Jesus utterly refused to contemplate such a war: His solution was that Israel should "turn away from desiring vengeance against Rome and destruction for the Gentiles, should meekly submit for the time being to servitude and injustice, and, trusting wholly to deeds of love and words of truth, should undercut pagan hostility, outmanœuvre political lordship, convert enemies to friends, and stand forth in the

[1] Cadoux, in loc. cit. p. 61.
[2] Windisch, *Der Mess. Krieg*, p. 95.

name and power of God as the heralds and propa-
gators of the one true religion."[1]

Why, we may ask, did Jesus thus renounce the
expected Messianic war? Not merely, we may be
sure, because He was convinced that such an appeal
was doomed to failure. He was obviously willing
to die for His cause. Why not in arms, if He knew
His cause to be just and believed that the war-
method might be right? Not even, as has often been
argued, because such action might seem to be a
presumptuous anticipation of the expected supernatural breaking-in of the Power of God, who was
Himself to "give the Kingdom".[2] The good Jew
never fought the less valiantly himself because he
believed that Yahweh alone could give the victory.[3]
No! so far as we can see, the refusal of Jesus to
wage war as Messiah was due first and foremost to
the fact that, in spite of all the precedents provided
by the Old Testament, He regarded the war-method
as inherently evil, a violation of His own supreme
commandment to love one's neighbour as oneself,
and a *reductio ad absurdum* of His basic principle that
the motive of all Christian discipleship is to be
"a son of your Father which is in heaven",[4] and so
to reflect in some poor measure the nature of the

[1] Cadoux, in loc. cit. pp. 61, 62.

[2] Luke xii. 32.

[3] It may, however, be noted that the apocalpytic expectations
both of Jesus and of the early Church have a real bearing on the
comparative silence of the Gospels concerning the applicability
of Jesus' ethic to social and political questions, a silence which
our opponents have not been slow to turn to account. "The
eschatological outlook . . . resulted in Christianity not
demanding the realization of its principles in society and State
for fear of destruction or failure. Had the first missionaries been
told that the world was to go on existing for long, long ages yet,
and that Christ would not return though centuries pass, they
would not have been able, with good conscience, to let the world
go on taking the course it did take." (Harnack, *Militia Christi*,
p. 50).

[4] Matt. v. 45.

God who "maketh His sun to rise on the evil and the good" alike.

(5) Thus to place the great sayings of Jesus against this wider background of the life of His nation is not to rob them of their higher spiritual qualities: it is only to insist that one cannot rightly interpret them till they are first set in their true historical perspective; and it is to discover additional point and colour in passage after passage. Even when the main bearing of a saying is upon the ordering of life within the Fellowship, there is an inevitable side-glance at the current national situation, and this very fact suggests that the sayings themselves are of wider application than is often admitted. For example:

(a) Though the chief importance of Jesus' Temptation is that it shows Him to us reaching the full realization of His "Sonship", and the conviction that for Him Messiahship must mean something very different from the popularly expected rôle, yet it is surely significant that Jesus defines to Himself the meaning of His mission by reference to the kind of dominion which He felt compelled to renounce: "The devil showeth him all the kingdoms of the world, and the glory of them; and he said unto him, All these things will I give thee, if thou wilt fall down and worship me."[1] If there be any force in the argument of this chapter, then at least at the beginning of His ministry Jesus *did* feel Himself called by God to exercise authority over the life of the nations *as such*, and not only to wield a purely spiritual rule in men's hearts; for wideworld rule over the nations was the Messiah's recognized destiny.[2] To refuse to "worship Satan" must then mean, not to renounce a national kingdom *simpliciter*, but to renounce "satanic" methods of winning that kingdom. What Jesus turned from, as morally

[1] Matt. iv. 8 f.   [2] Isa. lx. 3, etc.

wrong and disloyal to His vocation, was the one and only recognized way to empire in His own day, the way of the sword.

(b) Similarly, when Jesus sets up a new standard of greatness among His disciples with the words, "The rulers of the Gentiles lord it over them. . . . Not so shall it be among you,"[1] it is impossible to admit that He is not at the same time passing judgment on the kind of dominion exemplified by the pagan empire, a dominion won by warfare, exercised over unwilling subjects, and maintained by the power of armed force.

(c) The same background appears to lie behind the crucial sayings of the Sermon on the Mount. It has become a commonplace to assert that all the sayings in the section beginning, "Resist not him that is evil,"[2] are meant to govern the disciple in his private capacity, and leave untouched his duty as a member of society and of the nation. But this is hardly consistent with the facts that all three illustrations relate to *social* sanctions—the Lex Talionis which Jesus claims to transcend;[3] the right to justice in the public courts;[4] the liability to compulsory state labour. The last reference in particular—"whosoever shall compel thee to go one mile"[5]—vividly suggests the domineering bearing of the Roman or Herodian official. Indeed the background of the whole "non-resistance" section stares one in the face. Jesus' fellow-countrymen are to pursue the policy of reconciliation and peace with the foreign ruler, even at the risk of temporary submission to injustice.

[1] Mark x. 42–5.
[2] Matt. v. 38 ff.
[3] Matt. v. 38–9.
[4] Matt. v. 40, which Paul accepted as something more than a hyperbolical Semitic metaphor, as seems clear from 1 Cor. vi. 7.
[5] Matt. v. 41; literally "impress"; cf. Mark xv. 21 of Simon bearing the Cross.

(d) The same is true of the next paragraph containing the "love-your-enemy" sayings.[1] Once again it is commonly argued that the word "enemy" must be limited to the private enemy, or at any rate to the fellow-Jew-enemy.[2] The word used, it is pointed out, is not *polemios*, the foe in time of war, but *echthros*, one who stands in a relationship of personal hatred. This linguistic argument has little force, for *polemios* is nowhere used in the New Testament, whereas *echthros* is used both in the Septuagint and in the New Testament for the public as well as the personal enemy.[3] When we remember how Jesus extends the scope of the parallel word "neighbour",[4] it seems likely that He similarly enlarges the idea of an "enemy". If it be argued that the word "neighbour" in Leviticus xix. 18 (of which Matthew v. 43 is apparently an echo) is a technical term for a compatriot or fellow-Israelite, then it follows *a fortiori* that the command to love not only "neighbours" but "enemies" is a command not only to love compatriots even when enemies, but to love even the foreign enemy himself. The same inference may be drawn from the implied antithesis in verse 47, for "brethren" regularly means "fellow-Israelites", and suggests as its converse the "stranger" or "foreigner". Moreover all these sayings must be interpreted with reference to the environment in which they were presumably spoken; that is in Galilee, the hot-bed of revolutionary nationalism, where armed resistance to the hated dominion of the foreigner was the burning question of the hour. Are we to believe that Jesus, claiming Himself to be Messiah, had nothing to say concerning the bearing of these crucial sayings

[1] Matt. v. 43–8.
[2] See, e.g. Montefiore, *Synoptic Gospels*, Vol. II, p. 85.
[3] See Windisch, *Theol. Rundschau*, 1915, p. 345.
[4] Luke x. 29 ff.

upon this inter-racial enmity? Thus Professor Windisch again, though himself no Pacifist, can write: "When Jesus bade His followers love their enemies, do good to them, pray for them, endure their attacks and provocations with meekness . . . He stifled every thought of rebellion and national war"[1]; and, even in the heat of war-time, he feels compelled to admit that "it must not be overlooked that Pacifism, in applying the principles of the Gospel to the national enemy, seems better to agree with the spirit of Jesus".[2]

(e) Finally, many of the premonitions of national disaster, which the Gospels so often put upon Jesus' lips, take on a new and a much more vivid colour, once we realize that Jesus is contemplating, not only the penalty of rejecting His spiritual Gospel, but also the dire consequences which are bound to fall upon His people, if they prefer militant nationalism to His own pacifist policy of patience, peace, and reconciliation. We may instance the lamentation over Jerusalem[3]; the woes pronounced over the unrepentant Galilean towns[4]; the warning concerning the reading of the signs of the weather[5]; the advice to seize the first chance of reconciliation with one's adversary[6]; the urgent call to repentance, driven home by the reference to Pilate's brutal massacre[7]; the parable of the unfruitful fig-tree,[8] and of the wicked husbandmen[9]; the prediction of the destruction of Jerusalem[10]; and finally Jesus' ominous reply

[1] *Der Mess. Krieg*, p. 31.
[2] *Theol. Rundschau*, 1915, p. 346.
[3] Luke xix. 41-4.
[4] Matt. xi. 20 ff.; Luke x. 13 ff.
[5] Luke xii. 54 ff.
[6] Luke xii. 58.
[7] Luke xiii. 1 ff.
[8] Luke xiii. 6 ff.
[9] Mark xii. 1 ff.
[10] Mark xiii. 1 ff. and the parallels.

to the women who wept after Him on His way to
the Cross, ending with the words, "If they do these
things in the green tree, what shall be done in the
dry?"[1] Jesus unquestionably foresaw untold
disaster for His people as a result of their rejection
as a nation of His own pacifist ethic: and, doing so,
can He possibly have omitted to apply that ethic
explicitly to the national situation in His own day?

(6) The place of the Cross in Jesus' redemptive
purpose, and in the Christian doctrine of reconciliation and the conquest of evil, must be more fully
discussed in Chapter VI. But the Cross has first to
be considered as an event in history. And,
historically speaking, the Cross was the direct
consequence of Jesus' pacifist ethic alike in teaching
and in practice: in teaching, because His Pacifism
towards the Gentiles in general and Rome in
particular would undoubtedly arouse the patriotic
animus of the multitude, and so explain the sudden
waning of His popularity and His ultimate betrayal
to the authorities; in practice, because the same
principles which forbade rebellion against Rome also
forbade violent resistance to His enemies on Jesus'
own part. It was this that brought Jesus to the
Cross, while His own people yelled, "Not this man,
but Barabbas," preferring the champion of armed
revolution to the Lord of love.[2] The plain fact is
that, because Jesus was *not* a Barabbas, He went to
the Cross. It is probable indeed (to judge by such
passages as Mark viii. 31, Mark ix. 31 etc.) that for
some time before the crisis Jesus had already seen

---

[1] Luke xxiii. 27 ff.; "I understand the obscure closing sen-
tence to mean: If the Romans practise such cruelties as this
crucifixion of me when peace is flourishing, what atrocities will
they commit when it has withered away amid the storms of
war?" (Cadoux, in loc. cit. p. 64.)

[2] The word λῃστής, "robber", which is used of Barrabas in
John xviii. 40, is the word used most frequently by Josephus to
discribe the armed Zealot "revolutionaries".

what His fate was bound to be, so that the Cross
may well have presented itself to Him as the direct
alternative to the waging of the Messianic war.   By
dying, and not by the warlike methods of popular
expectation, would He proclaim to His nation His
conception of Messiahship.[1]

This, no doubt, is a line of argument from which
some will vigorously dissent.   Christ died on the
Cross, we are told, not as a result of His pacifist
ethic, but simply as the world's predestined
Redeemer; he died "in obedience to the require-
ments of God".   This may be perfectly true; but
we may not for that reason, by way of a facile
theological truism, take a short cut past the factors
which determined the Cross as an event in history.
Jesus knew it to be His vocation to lead men to God,
and to demonstrate His power to overcome evil, by
the preaching and the practice of an ethic of absolute
love.   He had set this before Himself as a definite
alternative to the waging of the universally expected
Messianic war.   And by His death, not on the battlefield but on a Roman Cross, He sealed and con-
summated that alternative.

If our reasoning has been valid, then we must
recognize that the principles which we have been
studying, integral and fundamental as they are to
Jesus' ethics, were consciously intended by Himself
to have an application far wider than has often been
admitted.   Politics, the State, international relations
all come within the orbit.   In particular it may be
suggested that an Historical Religion, at the centre

[1] "He would have ruined His mission if He had encouraged
the war-fever. The quickening of conscience which He invoked
would have been lost. But He took upon Himself the consequences of the decision which, in opposition to the national
ideal, He had arrived at. He endured, He suffered, He went to
His death. And in spite of the Jews He became the Messiah
triumphant. Without strife of arms, though He, too, was a
fighter, the Galilean had conquered." (Windisch, *Der Mess.
Krieg*, p. 80.)

of whose doctrine of reconciliation stands the Cross, can have no excuse for excluding from its ethics, national no less than individual, that distinctive method of confronting evil which brought about the occurrence of the Cross as an event in history. The Pacifism which led Jesus to the Cross is so integral a part of His whole attitude towards the life of individuals and of the nation alike, that it must also be recognized to be an integral part of any ethic which can in the full sense of the word be called Christian.[1]

[1] Dr. Cadoux concludes the article to which reference has been made thus: "The politics of Jesus were no mere incident or accident of His ministry; they were interwoven with the most central things in His Gospel. It was His politics, more than anything else, that brought about His death; and it was by and through the temporary defeat of death that His ultimate and eternal victory was won. That is why Christians believe His death to be the most central and important fact in history. But if they are right in so emphasizing the significance of His death, then surely the ethical principles, from which both the politics and the death resulted, ought to be emphasized as of central importance also."

V

THE "WRATH" OF GOD

At this point we pass from questions mainly of interpretation to those which are more strictly theological. And here we meet the challenge, which it has become fashionable for highly-placed ecclesiastics to fling at us, that Pacifism is a modern "heresy". On the face of it the charge is surprising, for "heresy" strictly speaking means false doctrine which has been formally condemned by the Church, whereas the facts are that the earliest Church was almost universally pacifist, and Christians have always assumed that it is not the pacifist, but rather the militarist, position which, from the Christian standpoint, requires to be defended as "under certain circumstances" justifiable. Yet Dr. Temple, Archbishop of York, has recently argued[1] that Pacifism is a recrudescence of three ancient Church heresies: "Manichaeism", because the Pacifist "makes a sharp contrast between spiritual and material forces, and holds that the material cannot be completely subordinated to the spiritual"; "Marcionism", because he holds "a view of the New Testament as so superseding the Old Testament as to abolish it"; and "Pelagianism", because he believes in "man's capacity apart from conversion and sanctification to obey the Counsels of Perfection . . . a view which regards man as capable by the action of his own will of living by love only." The first of these three "heresies" need not detain us, for if it is relevant at all it is so only to pure Tolstoyism (i.e. the complete renunciation of every kind of force), a creed which we believe to be an over-simplification

[1] *York Diocesan Leaflet*, 1935.

of our own particular problem[1]; and in any case it is surely not "heresy" to "deny that the use of matter for the indiscriminate murder of human beings is or can ever be a manifestation of the Spirit".[2] The other two charges, however, bring us to the heart of our problem and must be frankly faced; but perhaps we may first reformulate this charge of "heresy" in plain English under three counts:

Firstly, Pacifism misrepresents the character of God, and the revelation of Him in Jesus Christ, by slurring over the sterner side of the Divine nature;

Secondly, the Pacifist ethic unwarrantably exalts love at the expense of righteousness and justice;

Thirdly, Pacifism misinterprets the true significance of the Cross. We shall deal with the first of these three charges in the present chapter and with the other two in Chapter VI.

Firstly, then, it is argued that Pacifism gives a one-sided picture of the Divine nature.[3] Are there not, we are asked, certain aspects of God's character which may not be wholly revealed in th Person of Jesus Christ, and certain factors in God's way of dealing with evil which are not wholly evident in Jesus' way of meeting it as evidenced in the New Testament? And may we not therefore be justified, in certain circumstances, in departing from the love-ethic, for which a warrant has been found in the

---

[1] For this see C. E. Raven, *Is War Obsolete ?* pp. 150 ff.

[2] C. E. Raven, in *Reconciliation*, December, 1935, p. 321.

[3] "It is significant that when pacifists speak of war, they hardly ever speak of it in relation to the mind of God, but always in relation to the mind of Jesus. And in doing so they usually give a wholly one-sided representation of the character of Christ. The sterner aspect of Our Lord's character is omitted, and the gentle and gracious aspect of His character is emphasized. Yet we must remember that there was a very stern side to Our Lord's character. This ignoring of the stern aspect of the character of God lies behind a good deal of the heresy which troubles the Church in our time." (Isaac Jolly, *Pacifism at the Bar of Holy Scripture and History*, p. 21.)

New Testament—such departure even on occasion
taking the form of participation in war? In a word,
are we not entitled to stress God's "wrath" as well
as His love, to offer ourselves as the instruments of
His punitive as well as of His reconciling activity?
It is clear that there are really two questions here:
(1) What is the truth about this "sterner" side of
the Divine nature? What does the New Testament
mean when it speaks of the "wrath" of God?
(2) In any case is it competent for the Christian to
seek to imitate God on this side of His activity?

(1) First, then, what has the New Testament to
tell us about the sterner side of God's nature?
It is perfectly true that there are sayings of Jesus
which suggest His belief in a God of stern justice as
well as of infinite love. Does He not teach that there
is a place for terrible severity as well as for longsuffering forbearance in the Divine providence?
"Depart from me, ye cursed, into the eternal fire
which is prepared for the devil and his angels"[1];
"I tell you, I know not whence ye are; depart from
me, all ye workers of iniquity. There shall be
weeping and gnashing of teeth"[2]; "Whoso shall
cause one of these little ones that believe on me to
stumble, it is profitable for him that a great millstone
should be hanged about his neck, and that he should
be sunk in the depth of the sea"[3]; "Rather fear
Him which is able to destroy both soul and body in
hell."[4] We think, too, of expressions like "our God
is a consuming fire".[5] And through Paul's letters,
especially that to the Romans, there run like a
recurrent refrain references to the Divine "wrath";
"The wrath of God is revealed from heaven against

[1] Matt. xxv. 41.
[2] Luke xiii. 27 f.
[3] Matt. xviii. 6.
[4] Matt. x. 28.
[5] Heb. xii. 29, taken over, of course, from Deut. iv. 24.

all ungodliness and unrighteousness of men"[1];
"Thou treasurest up for thyself wrath in the day of
wrath and revelation of the righteous judgement of
God; who will render to every man according to his
works"[2]; "For which things' sake cometh the
wrath of God upon the sons of disobedience"[3];
"The wrath is come upon them to the uttermost."[4]
As we shall see, the crux of the problem is the correct
understanding of the meaning of this word "wrath".

Over and above the Scriptural evidence we are
quite fairly bidden by our critics to take account of
the witness both of nature and of history to the
stern retributory justice of God. Both these aspects
of the problem must be more fully dealt with below.
But first it will be well to lay down certain general
principles; and to begin with, as to our method of
approach. Instead of asking, "How are these
sterner elements in the Divine nature and Divine
activity to be explained consistently with the
revelation given in Jesus Christ?" we shall do better
to ask, "What are we to conceive to be the nature of
God's purpose in creation, and of His problem in
dealing with evil in general and human sin in
particular?"

Now from any theistic, not to say Christian,
standpoint, must we not define this purpose and this
problem as the creation of a moral universe of free
persons, and the bringing of these persons into a
right relationship both to their fellow-men and to
God Himself? Moreover, if men are to be so trained
and disciplined, and yet at the same time are to
remain free, it would appear that both in the
environment or "field of operations" in which this
education and development are to take place, and

[1] Rom. i. 18.
[2] Rom. ii. 5 f.
[3] Col. iii. 6; cf. Eph. v. 6.
[4] 1 Thess. ii. 16.

also in the working out of these mutual relationships, there must be elements and factors "independent", so to speak, of the immediate and moment-by-moment control of the will of God. That is to say, there may be, for example, catastrophes in the world of nature, and events in the field of history, which, while they happen within God's world and therefore must be said to be "permitted" by Him, yet cannot be ascribed to Him as the direct result of His immediate volitional purpose and activity. The necessity of this for the safeguarding of human freedom and human personality would appear to be less obvious in the world of nature than in the sphere of human relationships; yet it must be insisted that it holds good in both alike. This truth has nowhere been put better than by Professor H. H. Farmer: "From the human side, we may say that it is essential to man's status as a personal being and to his sense of the significance of his moral life, that he should be called upon to make choices and decisions which make a difference and are not merely play acting . . . that he should be able to refuse to do God's will . . . in such wise that his refusal involves that *pro tanto* God's will is not done. . . . It would seem to be necessary, therefore, that there should be *a world which in some way stands over against both the will of God and the will of the individual*, having significance for both as that in and through which co-operation can be attained, and genuine sonship on the part of the latter achieved. Or stating it from the divine side, we might say that . . . God was under necessity to set man in a world which in a sense was as yet uncreated, a world in which the full working out of His will would depend upon the responses and decisions of man. It is confirmation of this that those religious philosophies which have failed to insist on *the world of nature and history as having* significance for, and *a relative independence of, the will of God,* nearly always end in a thoroughly depersonalized conception of man's relationship to God. *Minimize the independence of the world, and nothing can save the independence of man.*"[1]

We may put this in other words by saying that in any moral universe consisting of free persons there must be room left for an impersonal law of cause and effect working itself out in a manner relatively independent of the personal and immediate "fiat" of the Divine will. And God must be held to "permit" this for the sake of the safeguarding of human freedom and the development of human personality. This principle ordains that consequences shall always follow acts, and in particular that tragic consequences shall follow certain gross infringements of the laws of God's moral universe. And this surely means that, over against the apparent "sternness" of a God who seems to castigate man with punitive retribution, must be set the fact that there are certain happenings for which God may be said to be responsible, not because He directly wills them, but only because they take place in a universe for which He is ultimately responsible, and which He permits to work itself out according to certain definite laws of cause and effect. This would seem to be the only valid solution of our problem on the basis of a theistic rather than a mechanistic conception of the universe.

Furthermore, this principle of cause and effect, functioning in a sense "independently" of God's immediate will, must hold good even in the spiritual realm, and in the most intimate relations of man

[1] H. H. Farmer, *The World and God*, p. 69; italics mine. The present discussion is, of course, grossly inadequate to the magnitude of the problem, but may serve to indicate the lines along which a solution may be sought. Much the best modern treatment of the problem of Providence is to be found in this book by Professor Farmer.

with man and man with God.[1] "The wages of sin
is death",[2] even though God "desireth not the
death of a sinner, but rather that he should turn
from his wickedness and live." This spiritual law
of cause and effect may be amplified by saying that,
not only does sin bring forth punishment, but almost
invariably sin also brings forth more sin. The moral
universe in which we live is so constituted that when
man asserts his independence of God, his right, if he
so wills, to live for self alone, then he finds that his
way of living tends to call forth a similar way of
living in other men.[3] We thus arrive at the paradox,
most important for our particular problem, that even
that which appears to be Divine punishment for sin—
and indeed is, inasmuch as God permits sin to reveal
its true nature by reproducing its natural results in
men's lives—may often itself have to be called sin.
Thus even the punishment of sin, in so far as it may
itself be sin, may and often does itself fall under
God's condemnation.

Does not this line of thought compel us to modify
our preconception of a stern and angry God meting
out merciless punishment to His sinful subjects?
For the Divine punishment, we have seen, is not to
be thought of as something external to the sinning,
but is to be found in the tragic fact that the regular
consequence of sin is to create its own punitive
consequences, which are often themselves sinful.
What, then, do we mean when we speak about

[1] "The man who sins must get the soul of a sinner. If a man
could sin and keep the soul of a saint and the bliss of a saint,
that would mean the end of all moral distinctions altogether.
It is quite impossible to see how a God of love or any other sort
of God can run life on any other terms than this of the strictest
consequence. By the reliability of consequence we live, and by
the discipline of it we learn our errors and find the truth which
makes free." H. H. Farmer, in *Reconciliation*, November, 1928,
p. 209 f.

[2] Rom. vi. 23.

[3] This thought would seem to underlie the saying, "All they
that take the sword shall perish by the sword"; Matt. xxvi. 52.

"punishment" inflicted by an "angry" God?
Simply that God's "anger" against sin is revealed
by the fact that He has set us down in the kind of
world where His love does not mechanically save
us from the consequences of our sin. As Principal
James Denney has put it, "The divine punishment
is the divine reaction against sin expressing itself
through the whole constitution or system of things
under which the sinner lives."[1] Thus there seems
to be no need to speak about God's "anger" and
"punishment" as if they implied direct and personal
retaliation by God upon the sinner. A Divine will
against sin there certainly is, revealed in the creation
of a moral order which inexorably attaches consequences to it. But we must not think of the
Divine "anger" as if God, so to speak, personally
reacted against the sinner with explosive ire and
"took it out of him" in punishment.[2]

This argument may have seemed somewhat
abstract and remote from the New Testament, and
yet it has a completely adequate New Testament
basis in the Pauline doctrine of "wrath", which we
must now examine in some detail.[3] In the opening
chapter of Romans Paul writes: "The wrath of
God is revealed from heaven against all ungodliness
and unrighteousness of men."[4] Does this mean that
God is "angry" with men in an immediate and
personal sense, and therefore brings down upon them
vengeance and retribution by a specific and
deliberate act of the Divine will? It has been
pointed out that, strangely enough, Paul never uses

[1] *The Christian Doctrine of Reconciliation*, p. 203.
[2] "What happens to the sinner is simply due to the fact that
a moral universe, created by a moral will, is true to itself and
affirms itself steadily to the personality which it is seeking
to educate into harmony with itself." (H. H. Farmer, in
Reconciliation, November, 1928, p. 210.)
[3] See an admirable note by C. H. Dodd in his Commentary on
Romans, in the *Moffatt New Testament Commentary*, pp. 20-4.
[4] Rom. i. 18.

the verb "to be angry" with God as its subject, though when speaking of "love" he uses not only the noun but the verb.[1] It is curious moreover that, although the word "wrath" occurs in Paul's writings no less than twenty-one times, the expression "wrath *of God*" occurs only three times.[2] Much more often Paul uses the word in a curiously impersonal manner; frequently he speaks absolutely about "*the* Wrath", almost as if it were a proper noun[3]; and in one passage in particular[4]—which means literally, "Is God unjust who *brings upon us* the Wrath?"—he uses with it a verb (ἐπιφέρειν) which, as Dodd says, suggests that "to Paul 'the Wrath' meant, not a certain feeling or attitude of God towards us, but some process or effect in the realm of objective facts."[5] From all this it seems clear that Paul does not think of God as being actively angry in quite the same immediate and personal sense as he thinks of Him as actively loving. Dodd points out that Paul is here in line with the Psalmists and Prophets: "It would be fair to say that in speaking of wrath and judgment the Prophets and Psalmists have their minds mainly on events, actual or expected, conceived as the inevitable results of sin; and when they speak of mercy, they are thinking mainly of the personal relation between God and His people. Wrath is the effect of human sin: mercy is not the effect of human goodness, but is inherent in the character of God." Similarly Paul, so far as he retains the idea of "wrath", does so, "not to describe the attitude of God to man, but to describe an inevitable process of cause and effect in a moral universe",[6] that is to say, the principle of

---

[1] E.g. Eph. ii. 4; 2 Thess. ii. 16.
[2] Rom. i. 18; Col. iii. 6; Eph. v. 6.
[3] Rom. iii. 5; v. 9; xii. 19; xiii. 5; 1 Thess. ii. 16.
[4] Rom. iii. 5.
[5] Dodd, op cit., p. 22.
[6] Dodd, *Romans*, p. 23.

retribution, relatively independent of God's immediate volition, which is inherent in such a universe—exactly the position which we had already tentatively reached.

That "wrath" for Paul does mean this working out of the law of cause and effect is suggested most clearly when he writes: "After thy hardness and impenitent heart thou treasurest up for thyself wrath in the day of wrath and revelation of the righteous judgment of God; who will render to every man according to his works."[1] And the further truth, noted above, that the retribution, though in a sense Divine punishment, may in itself involve sin, appears when Paul, immediately after his reference to the revelation of "the wrath of God", adds the words "wherefore God gave them up in the lusts of their hearts unto uncleanness".[2] It is worth noting here, with reference to our own particular problem, that both the effect of law in general and the punitive action of the civil magistrate in particular are defined as "wrath"; that is to say, so far as the law is the instrument of God and the civil magistrate His agent, they are so, not as agents of His immediate personal will, but because through both alike the working out of the inexorable principle of retribution is illustrated.[3]

If our argument thus far is valid, it provides a real safeguard against the undue exaggeration of the sterner side of the Divine nature. We may now very briefly apply these general principles in the realms of (a) nature, and (b) history.

(a) First then, is God to be held immediately responsible for the sternness and violence of nature,

[1] Rom. ii. 5 f.
[2] Rom. i. 24.
[3] Rom. iv. 15: "What the law produces is the Wrath," i.e. the process of sin followed by retribution. Rom. xiii. 4: the magistrate is "a divine agent bringing the penalty of Wrath upon the evil-doer".

which, it is suggested, are an indication of certain similar elements in God's own nature? Must we not take account of the fact that Scripture insists that God is the Creator of heaven and earth, and that in His "marvellous works" His own nature is shown forth?[1] And it is not only the kindly side of nature which is associated with God; not only is He the giver of corn and oil and wine, the One who sends down the rain in due season: He is also the Controller of nature on her destructive side. Now Pacifism, it is alleged, ignores this side of nature and the light it throws upon the character and the ways of God. For how cruel and violent nature can be, a world full of creatures evolved through the stern discipline of struggle, a world where earthquake and flood and pestilence deal with those creatures with a frightful and seemingly mechanical relentlessness, a catastrophic world, it sometimes seems, inhabited by combative creatures and governed by an awfully castigating God. What sort of a world is this in which to practise the ethic of absolute love? Can the God who created it and rules it Himself be a God of absolute love?

Well, what does Jesus say? Certainly He accepts nature as reflecting the will of God. The sparrow that falls to the ground and dies does not do so "without your Father".[2] But the amazing thing is that Jesus uses this to illustrate, not the sternness, but the absolute love of God. To Him there was no contradiction between natural catastrophe and a God of absolute love, surely because He realized, as we all must, that in a moral universe, whose end is to train human personalities to love one another, so far from natural calamity running counter to the governing principle of love, it must be an almost essential part of it. For how should men learn to

[1] Cf. for example Ps. cvii.
[2] Matt. x. 29.

love one another in any deep way, except in a world
where sometimes circumstances so challenge us that
we are thrown back on one another's sympathy and
protective care?[1] But it is a very different matter,
as we shall see later, to find in the fact of natural
calamity, as an element in God's training of us, a
justification of violent methods in our own
"chastisement" of one another.

It is suggestive to trace, particularly in Scripture,
the way in which, as religious ideas develop, men
have related natural calamity to the "wrath" of
God, and sought from it to draw deductions as to
His character. In the most primitive stages thunder
and earthquake will be regarded as direct manifesta-
tions of the Divine "Mystery", however it be
conceived, in its most vindictive and destructive
form. Once personification of natural forces takes
place, such phenomena are explained as signs of the
anger of personal gods. Thus in the earliest strata
of the Old Testament the anger of Yahweh is seen in
earthquake, pestilence and the like. But often it is
still an indiscriminate and irrational anger. "The
prophets took up this idea, but rationalized it by
teaching that disaster is not an outbreak of
irresponsible anger, but an expression of the outraged
justice of God. There is no disaster but deserved
disaster; . . . sin is the cause, disaster the
effect."[2] In Jesus we reach a stage at which even
this comparatively high level of thought is transcended. He clearly teaches that there *may* be
disaster which is *not* deserved disaster, and that
suffering is not necessarily a sign of the Divine

[1] "I do not see that the deeper exercises of love, heroic self-
sacrifice, tender protectiveness, mutual helpfulness, could ever
begin, much less grow, in a world where there were no final hazard
like that of death, and no trouble came to us at all except as a
just punishment for our sins." (H. H. Farmer, in *Reconciliation*,
November, 1928, p. 209.)

[2] Dodd, *Romans*, p. 22 f.

displeasure. "Those eighteen, upon whom the tower in Siloam fell and killed them, think ye that they were offenders above all the men that dwell in Jerusalem? I tell you, Nay."[1] "His disciples asked him, saying, Rabbi, who sinned, this man, or his parents, that he should be born blind? Jesus answered, Neither did this man sin, nor his parents, but that the works of God should be made manifest in him."[2] That is to say, men may undergo suffering which has no relation whatever to their deserts: yet once we grasp the aim and end of the Divine purpose in their lives, we shall see that everything may be comprehended within the all-embracing love of God.

Finally, when we say that God is "responsible" for this undeserved suffering, we must do so always remembering that (in line with the general principles already laid down) there is a sense in which the world of nature must be thought of as relatively independent over against the immediate will of God. So far as catastrophe is "an act of God" it is not an ethical act, but rather what might be called a "cosmic" act, for which God is responsible only in the sense that it takes place within a world created by Him; and as such it is no real indication of God's ethical character, and no real contradiction of His absolute love. Each happening in the world of nature is not to be ascribed to the direct initiative of God. Rather may He be thought of as the ground of this whole moral order, which has been created for His purpose and is eternally being preserved to carry out His ends.

(b) The same considerations hold good in any attempt to trace the will of God in history. Nothing, of course, is more characteristic of the Old Testament than its recognition that in history are to be found

[1] Luke xiii. 4 f.
[2] John ix. 2 f.

the best illustrations, not only of God's love, but also of His righteous "wrath". Indeed the Prophets read Israel's history as a constant disciplining by God of His people. We think of Isaiah's indictment of Israel's sin in a poem with the refrain, "For all this His anger is not turned away, but His hand is stretched out still."[1] Moreover, God uses human instruments to carry out His judgments: "Ho, Assyrian, the rod of mine anger, the staff in whose hand is mine indignation."[2] "The Lord that saith of Cyrus, He is my shepherd, and shall perform all my pleasure . . . whose right hand I have holden, to subdue nations before him."[3] God raises up enemies to oppress His people, and then, when He has done with these weapons, He breaks them also and casts them away: "Come, behold the works of the Lord, what desolations he hath made in the earth; he breaketh the bow and cutteth the spear in sunder; he burneth the chariots in the fire. Be still, and know that I am God."[4]

What is the Christian Pacifist to say to all this? Doubtless we shall point out that, just as in the case of nature, so in that of history the Hebrew thought naïvely about the activity of God and the manifestation of His "wrath". But, even so, as Christians we cannot acquiesce in any view that bows God out of His own world and denies that there is a Divine Providence at work in history. We shall also perhaps console ourselves that probably the plainest of all the lessons which the Old Testament teaches us from history is that God works out His purpose through a "remnant", a minority ready to think and act ahead of the community as a whole, and so

[1] Isa. xix. 12, 17, 21.
[2] Isa. x. 5.
[3] Isa. xliv. 28 f.
[4] Ps. xlvi. 8–10.

F

to keep alive the vision of God's redemptive way. But the argument remains, and must be frankly faced, that history sometimes seems to show war to be a divinely sanctioned way of meeting and overcoming evil. Even if our opponents waive their right of appeal to the "righteous" and "God-approved" wars of the Old Testament, not to speak of modern times, they can still argue that war, though the consequence of human sin, is also the divinely permitted remedy for sin. Measured against the absolute perfection of the ethic of the Kingdom of God war may never be right: but, since man is a fallen creature, it may be relatively right in God's sight, and as such a necessary and legitimate expression of one side of the Divine nature. Have we any answer to this?

Following the general principles laid down in this chapter, we shall reply that, just as there are elements in the world of nature, so are there elements in the world of history which, if the freedom of human personality is to be safeguarded, must be considered to be relatively independent of the immediate will of God. There thus may be much in history which cannot legitimately be claimed as a revelation either of the will of God or of His essential nature. "It is not unimportant to realize", writes Professor Farmer, "that to speak of a general revelation of God in *all* nature and history is . . . almost a contradiction in terms." "The notion that faith should be able to discern the active presence of God in all events and all situations is merely pietistic; it is neither supported by experience nor necessitated by the thought of God and His intercourse with man."[1] It is true, of course, that nothing can be held to be entirely outside the sphere of Divine Providence, since God cannot be other than the Lord of His world; but this does not permit us to

[1] *The World and God*, pp. 85, 90.

take any particular line of human activity, either in the past or in the present, and withdraw it from the scope of the principle that human freedom is permitted and retribution follows human sin, as if we were then entitled to say, "This is, or was, the Lord's doing". We are not reduced to a choice between a theory of blind chance and the theory that every separate event must be ascribed to the immediate will of God. There is a third possibility, namely that God does not directly cause the separate events, but that they do all lie within the all-embracing power and wisdom of His providence.

Furthermore, when we recall that the result of sin is commonly to bring forth not only punishment but also more sin, so that sin is chastened by sin, new light falls upon some of the seemingly strange ways of God in history, as for example when He is said to use the ruthless methods of the heathen Cyrus for the punishment of His own people.[1] Here is the "wrath" of God making even evil subserve His purpose, so that "surely the wrath of man shall praise thee".[2] The punishment of sin by sinful men using sinful methods can in this sense be God's punishment, but the methods do not thereby cease to be sinful, nor can God be held to will or to sanction such methods for our imitation. We are, of course, merely groping on the edge of an impenetrable mystery, and we may venture once again to quote Professor Farmer, whose book has been found so helpful in this discussion: "That events should be really the result of the interplay of intramundane causes, including the choices of beings who are free to resist God, and yet also be controlled and directed by His manifold wisdom and sovereign will; that God has a purpose which He is working out in history . . . yet which, being God's

[1] Isaiah xliv. 28 f.
[2] Ps. lxxvi. 10.

purpose, transcends history altogether so that man cannot interpret it adequately in terms of this life; that in spite of all the confusion and heartbreak and frustration of life . . . every individual may, if he will, not in imagination but in fact, rest upon a love which numbers the very hairs of his head—that is a conception before which the intellect sinks down in complete paralysis. It is only possible to maintain because in the religious awareness something deeper than intellect is involved."[1]

(2) We are now in a position to answer the second half of our original question. Even granted that there is indeed a "sterner" side to the Divine nature, is it ever competent for the Christian, in his ethical dealings with his fellows, to seek to imitate God on this side of His activity? Enough has been said to indicate how perilous would be such an assumption. Turning now to the New Testament we may make these preliminary observations:

(a) True to the Old Testament, Jesus evidently regards punitive justice as being specifically a function of God Himself, not to be usurped by man: "Shall not God avenge His elect, which cry to Him day and night, and He is longsuffering over them?"[2] And Paul strikes exactly the same note: "Avenge not yourselves, beloved, but give place unto wrath (i.e. stand aside and allow God's 'Wrath' to have its way): for it is written, Vengeance belongeth unto me; I will recompense, saith the Lord." Then immediately there follows the great Pacifist watchword: "But if thine enemy hunger, feed him; if he thirst, give him to drink: for in so doing thou shalt heap coals of fire upon his head. Be not overcome of evil, but overcome evil with good."[3]

---

[1] *The World and God*, p. 100 f. I wish also to acknowledge much helful suggestion, both in this section and the next, from conference with several friends, in particular Prof. Norman W. Porteous, Rev. Oliver Dryer, and Rev. A. C. Craig.
[2] Luke xviii. 7.   [3] Rom. xii. 19–21.

(b) Though, as we have seen, Jesus certainly does not close His eyes to the stern side of the Divine nature, yet it is *the other side* which is always held up to men for imitation, if they are to be "sons of the Father", that is to say reflect in their own conduct that which is truly characteristic of God: "Love your enemies, and pray for them that persecute you; that ye may be sons of your Father which is in heaven: for he maketh his sun to rise on the evil and the good, and sendeth rain on the just and the unjust."[1]

(c) As has been suggested in a previous chapter,[2] in this matter of the right to inflict penalty the gulf between God and man is so great that we cannot regard Divine methods of justice, even when parabolically illustrated from human life by Jesus Himself, as *ipso facto* approved by Jesus for human imitation. We cannot possibly argue from God's way to what ought to be man's way until we have shown that the enormous dissimilarity between God and man makes no difference. Our duty as Christians is not to imitate God, but first to realize God's redemptive purpose towards ourselves, and secondly so to act towards our fellows as to make credible and effective that way of God as revealed in Jesus Christ.

To turn now to more specific questions concerning this suggested "imitation" of God:

(a) If God in nature can use destructive violence and yet remain loving, may not we do so also, even to the extent of war? Does the fact of natural catastrophe, as an element essential in God's training of us, provide any justification of violent methods in our dealings with one another? Surely not. For the one justification we were able to find for the unkindliness of the natural world was that it does as

[1] Matt. v. 44 f.
[2] See p. 32.

a matter of fact teach men to love one another and
provide opportunities for mutual help.   It may be
argued, no doubt, that war does, at least as one of
its by-products,[1] have the same noble consequences.
But it would be preposterous to claim that generally
speaking war educates the human race in love and
fellowship and mutual helpfulness.   On the contrary
it is both the product and the cause of hatred and
division and mutual destructiveness.   The question
appears closed when we remember that natural
calamity has been shown to be a "cosmic" rather
than an ethical act of God, and that there cannot
possibly be any human parallel to such "cosmic"
activity.[2]

(b) Because God permits the working out of a
moral law of cause and effect in the punishment of
sin, must we not, however unwillingly, acquiesce in
men suffering for our sins and their own, and indeed
consent to play our part in the punishment of those
sins?   May not war, for example, be regarded as
society co-operating with God in affirming the moral
order?   Such an argument seems to me undoubtedly
to justify certain restrictive and even forcible social
sanctions.   Just as God's universe has laws which
react against the evil-doer, so must our society have
laws which similarly react and similarly demand
penalties.   Otherwise no moral order of society
could exist.   But what do we really mean when we
speak about "affirming the moral order"?   Presumably we mean "demonstrating it to be what in
point of fact it is".   And if, as the Christian

---

[1] For this see pages 104 ff, below.

[2] "Obviously you cannot argue straight away from the Deity
making a suitable cosmic setting for the education of the race
in love to one or two members of that race dealing with one
another. Obviously the fact that One is the Supreme Educator
and the others a few of the very immature educatees makes all
the difference." (H. H. Farmer, in *Reconciliation*, November,
1928, p. 209.)

believes, the moral order is one whose basic principle is love, then only such social sanctions are justifiable as shall result in just such a demonstration; that is to say, they must be ultimately not merely punitive but "redemptive", designed to win men back from evil to good by evoking from them a response to the appeal of love. Any sanction which in its essential nature contradicts this principle is wrong: and *that is why war is wrong*. We shall never "affirm" to a man that the moral order in which we live is one of love by blowing him in pieces with high-explosive, however clearly we may have first represented to him that our action is the inevitable consequence of his own previous wrong-doing. This line of thought must be more fully developed in the next chapter.

(c) Because in history God has apparently used human instruments for the accomplishment of His righteous will, as for example in the case of Cyrus, are we therefore justified in regarding ourselves, and even offering ourselves, as the agents of God's punitive retribution—once again even to the extent of war? That might seem to be human logic. And yet this is surely just one of those situations in which Paul sometimes felt compelled to call a halt to the arguments of human logic with a "God forbid!"[1] There are some conclusions which it would be a sin against the Gospel of God's love to draw. God Himself may be able to do or "permit" certain things, which men can never do, without stultifying His ultimate aim of redemption, because God is Holy and we are not. And in order to "affirm the moral order" of love even God had to add to His inexorable law of retribution, and to His human agents for the chastisement of sin, a Saviour who came and bore in His own Person the worst consequences of sin, and broke the vicious circle of cause and effect by

[1] E.g. Rom. iii. 4, 6, 31 etc.; Gal. ii. 17 etc. I owe this thought to Prof. Porteous.

leading men to repentance. And that is why—quite apart from the fact that there is in truth no punitive activity of God which we *can* imitate, seeing that God's punishment is "Wrath" in the sense already defined, to which there is no possible human parallel —our duty in this connection is not to try to imitate God. Our duty is rather to point men to God's "redemptive" way, and so to act towards our fellows as to make that Divine way credible. The faith of the Christian Pacifist is that war is the greatest of all stumbling-blocks in the way of belief in the credibility and effectiveness of God's redemptive method of overcoming evil, as He has revealed it to us in Jesus Christ, and that the refusal to meet force with force would do more than anything else to make the Gospel credible to a world in bondage to cynicism and fear. We men cannot set ourselves up as petty gods seeking to "imitate" certain mysterious cosmic functions of the Divine activity; we can imitate the way of Jesus, who, even though it were admitted that He does not fully reflect *all* the attributes of God, does by His teaching and example give us all the guidance necessary for the ordering of our relations with our fellow-men.

VI

THE LAW, THE GOSPEL, AND THE CROSS

IN the last chapter we dealt with the charge that
Christian Pacifism fails to do justice to the sterner
side of the Divine nature. A second count in the
charge of "heresy" is that Pacifism unduly exalts
the Gospel of love at the expense of righteousness and
law. Sometimes the charge is made on the ground
of an alleged misinterpretation of Scripture, as for
example when Dr. Temple accuses Pacifists of the
"Marcionite" error of so interpreting the New
Testament that it wholly supersedes the Old. But
there is a Gospel vein in the Old Testament also.
Even as far back as the eighth century we meet
Hosea, the prophet of God's love; and as Israel
advances towards a truer understanding of God, her
thinkers pass beyond the crude "justice" of the
books of Joshua and Judges to the profoundly
"Christian" standpoint of the book of Jonah;
"Doest thou well to be angry? . . . Thou hast
had pity on the gourd . . . and should not I
have pity on Nineveh, that great city?"[1] On any
modern understanding of the relation of the Old
Testament to the New, and of the growing revelation
of God and His purpose which we have in both, it
must surely be admitted that the method of the Law,
as set out in the Old Testament, is a noble but an
essentially pre-Christian and sub-Christian attempt
to point the way to a right relationship between man

[1] Jonah iv. 9-11.

and God and between man and man, and that in the
New Testament there is revealed to us "a more
excellent way".[1] It is as *Christians* and not
otherwise that we accept the Old Testament as well
as the New Testament as God's Word, and we are
therefore entitled to take to the interpretation of the
Old Testament the insight which has come to us
from the New. For this we have sufficient warrant
in Jesus' own words, "Ye have heard that it was
said to them of old time, ... But I say unto
you ".[2] It is because Jesus Christ came that the
Old Testament still makes sense. We have Jesus'
warrant, too, for believing in a progressive revelation
of God's ways, as men grow in their capacity to
understand them, and for the conviction that certain
aspects of truth, only implicit even in Jesus' own
teaching, are bound to become more and more
explicit to the Christian conscience under the
guidance of the Holy Spirit: "I have yet many
things to say unto you, but ye cannot bear them
now. Howbeit when he, the Spirit of truth, is
come, he shall guide you into all the truth ; . . .
for he shall take of mine, and shall declare it unto
you."[3]

But the argument usually takes a more theological
form ; the Law, it is asserted, must always precede
the Gospel, and remain as its indispensable foundation. Again we may quote Dr. Temple: "Sound
doctrine and experience alike assure us that the
stage of the Law must precede that of the Gospel,
and that, though the Gospel carries us far beyond
the Law, we need the foundation provided by the
Law to be secure before we can truly respond to the
Gospel. . . . It was to a people long disciplined
by the Law that the Gospel was proclaimed." Just

[1] 1 Cor. xii. 31.
[2] Matt. v. 21 f.
[3] John xvi. 12 ff.

how easily such an argument can be turned to
account by the militarist will be seen if we re-write
it in militarist terms, as has been done by Professor
C. E. Raven, who himself, of course, dissents:
"Justice is the essential preliminary to peace; and
justice can be established only on the basis of
acknowledged law. In human history Moses preceded Jesus, and it was upon the foundation of
legalism that the superstructure of the Gospel was
built. We must proceed by the same sequence.
The machinery already exists; and if another
generation has to be immolated before it can be set
to work, the sacrifice may be inevitable and justified
by its results. Let us prepare for another war to
end war."[1]

Now Dr. Temple's statement just quoted, though
it contains of course a large measure of truth, is also
quite dangerously misleading. If he is right in
insisting that the Law must always precede the
Gospel and must remain as its permanent foundation, then not only must the argument of most of
Paul's Epistles go by the board, but the Apostle
had no right to presume to proclaim the Gospel to
Gentiles without first thoroughly training them under
the discipline and the sanctions of the Law. It is
the very essence of New Testament teaching that the
grace of God in the Gospel is operative towards men
who are unrighteous and not yet obedient to the
Law's discipline: "God commendeth His own love
towards us, in that, *while we were yet sinners*, Christ
died for us."[2] It has been the evangelical experience
of all the great Christian saints from St. Paul down-
wards to be reduced to despair just because they
could not obey the Law and thus "qualify" for the
Gospel; and it is the experience of all Christian
teachers that it is fruitless to try to inculcate the

[1] C. E. Raven, in *Reconciliation*, March, 1936, p. 60.
[2] Rom. v. 8.

Christian ethic before the heart has been changed
by the Gospel of the grace of God.[1]

In reply to the charge that Christian Pacifism, by
exalting the Gospel of absolute love, dethrones the
conception of law and justice taken over by Jesus
Himself from the Old Testament "Law" and
"Prophets", and thereby undermines the very
foundations of righteousness, we may now note the
following points in greater detail:

(1) Jesus' new and distinctive ethic, *and in
particular the definitely pacifist features in it*, is
specifically stated by Himself to have as its aim not
the "destruction" but the "fulfilment" of the Law.
The whole section begins with the statement:
"Think not that I came to destroy the law or the
prophets: I came not to destroy, but to fulfil."[2]
And at the end of the section we have the "non-
resistance" and "love-your-enemy" sayings as the
culminating illustrations of what Jesus means by
"fulfilling the law". To "fulfil the law" in Jesus'
thought evidently means to "give the full content"
to the older conception of Law, "to draw out its
underlying intention", "to make explicit that
which hitherto has been only implicit". Just how
His pacifist ethic achieves this we shall discuss in a
moment. Meantime it is important to note that
Jesus Himself, though definitely claiming to modify
and in a sense even to supersede the Law, just as
definitely denies that He is "destroying" it.

[1] "The Gospel is not a postscript to Christian ethics, but their
presupposition and preface; the love of God in the Gospel
precedes the righteousness which it makes possible, and not
vice versa. . . . If the foundation of Law had to be secure
before we can truly respond to the Gospel, Christianity is a fair-
weather religion, and its distinctive ethic cannot get started at all
until it is no longer needed. If you must not begin to love your
enemies until there are none, Christ's command is rendered
meaningless." (J. S. Whale, in *Reconciliation*, April, 1936,
p. 93.)
[2] Matt. v. 17.

Paul, too, frankly admits that in large measure the Gospel, when rightly understood, has superseded the Law—but always in the sense not of "destroying" the Law, but of accomplishing that at which the Law aimed, but failed to achieve.[1] We are guilty of "heresy", not when with Paul himself we recognize and insist upon this kind of supersession of the Law by the Gospel, but when like Marcion and Dr. Temple himself we set the way of justice and the way of love in so sharp an antithesis as to suggest that when we choose the one we necessarily "destroy" the other. Neither Jesus' teaching nor Paul's means that justice has been dethroned by love; it does mean that all human relationships must ultimately be based on the Gospel of love; that justice truly "fulfilled" is an outcome of love, rather than love a mere by-product of justice; that if we aim at love we shall establish justice by the way; that we can in fact secure justice only when we aim primarily not at it, but at the love out of which it springs. Paul feels the same about peace: like love it is one of the "fruits of the Spirit",[2] the reward of a whole way of life, to be attained not by aiming at "peace" alone, but as one of the "by-products of a larger quest".[3]

(2) Before we ask how the pacifist ethic of Jesus does actually thus "fulfil" or, to use more modern language, "sublimate" the conception of law and righteousness, it will be well to recall what was said above[4] about "affirming the moral order". Jesus does not think, as do we too often with our academic ways of thought, of a "moral order" in the abstract, which evil, again in the abstract, has invaded, and which has to be "vindicated" by resistance to evil

---

[1] *Romans* throughout, especially Chapters VII and VIII.
[2] Gal. v. 22.
[3] The phrase is Raven's: *Reconciliation*, March, 1936, p. 61.
[4] P. 86 f.

as a thing *per se*. That is to use legal and political analogies, and results in the misconception that God is concerned with abstract "law" rather than with persons, and that His chief end is to "vindicate the moral order of the universe", and to "uphold His own righteousness", rather than to fulfil His purpose of redemption towards mankind. Jesus on the other hand is dealing always, not with such an abstract "moral order", but with a world consisting of persons in relation to one another and to God; and in such a world justice can be truly "vindicated", and God's own righteousness "upheld", not by the mere restraint and punishment of evil, but only by making evil persons see the sinfulness of their ways,[1] through the employment of a redemptive method which will change the evil will, and restore right personal relationships, "so making peace".[2] For peace in the international sphere also depends upon something much more than the restraining of an "aggressor" or the vindication of a "righteous cause". Peace depends upon right relations between persons, upon mutual confidence in the common honesty, upon co-operation by all for the

---

[1] The common fallacy here in much of our thinking is that "the moral order, as inherent in the divine justice, appears as something standing over against the individual's inner life, capable of affirming itself and achieving its sovereign rights whether the inner life is redeemed or not." "But what if the moral order be, in the last analysis, nowhere save in the purposes and volitions of persons in relation to one another? In that case only in so far as those purposes and volitions are not merely checked and defeated, but also recreated into what they ought to be, can the moral order be said to be victorious in any sense that really matters. For only then will it have reaffirmed itself at the precise point where it has been negated and denied. We affirm, then, that a moral order which merely checks and annuls is not one which has at the heart of it an absolute valuation of the individual person as such; it is not the sort of moral order which is known to the Christian in and through his reconciliation to God through Christ." (H. H. Farmer, *The World and God*, pp. 252, 249 f.)

[2] Eph. ii. 15.

service of all, upon something far deeper than mere justice in the abstract, however ingeniously worked out by international "formulae". There can be no peace in any sphere at all which is not also what Paul calls "the peace of God which surpasses all human ingenuity".[1]

(3) How, then, does Jesus' pacifist ethic redeem the will from evil to good, restore right personal relationships, and thus truly "fulfil" and sublimate the Law? It does so because it offers, not merely negative passivity in the face of wrong, but an alternative, positive, and redemptive method of overcoming evil which renders all violent and punitive methods obsolete. The injunction to non-resistance,[2] which is so often taken to represent the whole pacifist ethic, is immediately followed by the positive commandment of all-embracing love. Retributive justice, which merely checks and punishes evil, is supplanted by active and self-sacrificial love, which redeems and changes the evil will, so "vindicating righteousness" in the only true sense of the word, and thereby "fulfilling the Law". This, and not mere non-resistance, must always be the foundation of the Pacifist position when adopted on specifically Christian grounds. For the Christian, if he renounces war, will do so, not because he denies that to react against evil by way of war may sometimes be better than not to react at all, but because he is convinced that to use such methods is equivalent to trying to cast out devils by Beelzebub the prince of devils,[3] and must stultify at the outset every effort to make credible and effective this alternative and positive method of sacrificial and redemptive love, to which as a disciple of the Crucified he is called.

---

[1] Phil. iv. 7: again the phrase is Raven's; *Reconciliation*, March, 1936, p. 61.
[2] Matt. v. 39.   [3] Matt. xii. 24.

It is unnecessary to repeat here what was said in Chapter III about how Jesus in His own Person and by His own example proved again and again the power of active love to overcome the evil in men's lives. And in the Cross the method of non-resistance finds its complete and final illustration, and the redemptive way of sacrificial love its perfect example. For Jesus deliberately willed to endure the Cross rather than prove false to His chosen redemptive way, believing that He and His could overcome the evil in men only by being willing to suffer to the uttermost rather than betray that way; and at Calvary we see Him laying down life rather than take it, in His own Person meeting the wickedness of violent men, Himself bearing sin's utmost penalty, the Just for the unjust, and yet overcoming that sin by the power of active, forgiving love. It is important, too, to remember that Jesus never sought to avoid the application of these principles because that way might lead to suffering and danger for others as well as for Himself. He never promised immunity even from death itself to those who accepted His way: "If any man would come after me, let him . . . take up his cross, and follow me."[1] When He "stedfastly set His face to go to Jerusalem",[2] He risked His followers' lives as well as His own. If He had been swayed by considerations of their safety, there would have been no Cross. But there would also have been no Resurrection, and no releasing into the world of the redemptive power of love.

What is it that gives to the Cross, and to the whole way of life of which it is the symbol, this unique "redemptive" power, that is the power to defeat evil by changing the evil will and winning it to good? I know of no finer statement than this: "God's

[1] Mark viii. 34.
[2] Luke ix. 51.

purpose is to win men's hearts to Himself. . . .
Obviously there is only one method of winning such
a victory when methods of force are ruled out, and
that is simply to love; to love so passionately, so
utterly, that even the most brutal and seemingly
triumphant violence of sin leaves it still love,
unchanged except in the increasing agony of its
disappointed desire to bless and to redeem. The
only qualification for victory required of love is that
it should be able to endure its most shattering defeat
and yet still remain love. If it does that, it has still
got the whip hand; for in its very weakness of
defeat it has within it the invincible strength of
remaining itself, and it will yet win its victory. As
someone has said, 'You cannot defeat defeat'.
. . . Let men take every advantage of the
seeming weakness of love, let them bruise and batter
and seek utterly to smash it, as they did at the
Cross; but let it still remain love, and in the end
they will have to give up, and look upon what their
hands have done, and break down in its presence.
At some time or other the very weakness of love will
cut them to the centre of their being with more
power than a two-edged sword—only it will be
spiritual power. I am sure that is so, human hearts
being what they are. The weakness of a God of love
is stronger than men."[1]

We shall no doubt be met with the rejoinder that
only a sentimentalist would dream of trying to apply
the method of redemptive love to international
affairs. This is what Dr. Temple apparently has in
mind when he accuses Pacifists of a "Pelagian"
heresy. "Man," he writes,[2] "is incapable of living
by love unless the grace of God has both converted
and sanctified him; so that the law of love is not
applicable to nations consisting in large measure of

[1] H. H. Farmer, *Things not Seen*, p. 32 f.
[2] *York Diocesan Leaflet*, 1935.

G

unconverted or (as is the case of most, if not all, of us) very imperfectly converted citizens." We would prefer to believe that Dr. Temple only means that the perfectly converted alone can love perfectly, and not, as might appear at first sight, that the way of love can be effective only when directed towards the perfectly converted. For to say that love has a saving and redeeming power only when directed towards the wholly converted and sanctified is surely a denial of the whole of the New Testament. If the last part of Dr. Temple's statement is true in that sense, then both Jesus and Paul were manifestly sadly at fault. The Jews were a very imperfectly converted nation in Jesus' own day, yet "God so loved the world that he gave his only Son,"[1] and Jesus so loved His people that He died for them at Calvary. Was His Cross after all inapplicable? Was Paul merely presumptuous when he preached "a more excellent way"[2] to folk at Corinth who were still heathen? Was he deceiving himself when he wrote "God commendeth his own love toward us, in that, *while we were yet sinners*, Christ died for us"?[3] But, taking Dr. Temple's words as they stand, his inference apparently is that in matters affecting the relations of nation with nation the Church must be content to fall into line with the State in reverting to a sub-Christian ethic. A more legitimate inference would surely be that the Church must refuse to collaborate with the State in so far as the State still finds itself unable or unwilling to apply an ethic which is binding on the Church. "Love is not applicable to nations," says Dr. Temple, "therefore Christians, when they act as members of their nations, are not bound by the law of love." "No!" replies the Christian Pacifist, "if nations cannot or will not act as Christians should, then Christians cannot conform to what the nation does." If this

[1] John iii. 16.   [2] 1 Cor. xii. 31.   [3] Rom. v. 8.

alternative is, as Dr. Temple asserts, "heresy", many of us would insist that his own alternative is just as surely "apostasy".

The third and last count in the charge of heresy is that the line of thought which we have been following misinterprets the true significance of the Cross, and this in three ways:

(1) First, it is alleged, the Christian Pacifist ignores the fact that the Cross is *theologically unique*. "Our Lord's death upon the Cross had relations and meanings to which nothing in our life corresponds. He died on the Cross as the World's Redeemer. This is the great message of the New Testament regarding His death."[1] Though in large measure true, such a statement is just as perilous as are all half-truths. Similarly, it might be argued with much truth that Jesus, as only Son of God, had a sense of vocation also entirely unique, and a redemptive aim and purpose with which that of even the noblest of His martyr followers is in no wise comparable. This is the whole force of such sayings as, "Christ also suffered for sins *once*, the righteous for the unrighteous, that he might bring us to God",[2] or, "we have been sanctified through the offering of the body of Jesus Christ *once for all*".[3] This is a sacrifice never to be repeated and never emulated. Moreover, we are reminded, Jesus Himself seems to have fully realized that there was something unique in the setting of His self-sacrifice both in time and in place. Hence the constant references to "His hour".[4] "It is to be recognized that there

---

[1] Isaac Jolly, *Pacifism at the Bar of Holy Scripture and History*, p. 18.

[2] 1 Pet. iii. 18.

[3] Heb. x. 10.

[4] This is, of course, chiefly in the Fourth Gospel, and may perhaps be held to reflect the point of view rather of the Apostolic Church than of Jesus Himself. See John ii. 4; vii. 30; viii. 20; xii. 23; xii. 27; xiii. 1; xvii. 1.

was a place and a time which alone would suit the purpose of His suffering, so that man might understand it and take it to his heart and conscience. Other hands would inflict it, but only when He chose to exercise His determining power to give or to withhold. The narratives make it plain that Simon Peter's public recognition furnished a signal that His hour was at hand, since the Church's foundation of faith confessed had at last been laid as a living rock. Till the hour came which alone accorded with the fulfilment and secure recognition of His redemptive aim He had withdrawn, again and again, from the grasp of His enemies, thus plainly showing that suffering and death were not of themselves sufficient apart from adequate recognition. But in Jerusalem, at a Passover season, in full view alike of disciples, people and rulers, He found His hour and His altar, and as a Lamb suffered Himself to be led to the Sacrifice, a Paschal offering, a Ransom for many."[1] Jesus' unique redemptive purpose, the choice—not to say predestined appointment—of both time and place, gives His sacrifice a redemptive efficacy which does not in any comparable manner belong to the "method of sacrificial love", when adopted by His disciples as a professed and regular manner of life.

Now all this is admittedly and gloriously true. And yet the manner chosen by Jesus to fulfil His redemptive purpose must surely have been in line with His whole daily manner of life, and must have owed its efficacy precisely to that consistency. His final victory over evil on the Cross cannot have been by means inconsistent with those by which He won daily victories over evil in the men and women with whom He came into contact. His triumph over sin cannot have been won by a method out of harmony and incomparable with that method by which He bade His disciples overcome evil when they met it

[1] I owe this fine statement to my friend Principal W. A. Curtis.

in their fellows. In other words, to amend our previous quotation: "Our Lord's death on the Cross had relations and meanings to which *a very great deal in our life corresponds.*" Paul himself, though he constantly emphasizes the uniqueness of Christ's sacrifice, insists, too, that the Christian must be "crucified with Christ", if the Cross of Calvary is to have any efficacy for him.[1]

Moreover if it be true, as we believe it is, that Jesus throughout His whole ministry was seeking "a place and a time which alone would suit the purpose of His suffering"; if it be true that it was the hour of the Cross which "accorded with the fulfilment and secure recognition of His redemptive aim"; and if it is these truths which give to the Cross its peculiar characteristics and its redemptive quality—then it must also be true that the Cross was the goal towards which Jesus' purpose more and more consciously moved throughout His entire ministry. And if the Cross had this central place in Jesus' whole Messianic consciousness, then we have no right to isolate it as a theological mystery which has no bearing on the ethic which He taught or the personal decisions which He made. Indeed we seem to be driven back to our previous conclusion that Jesus, knowing Himself to be Messiah, knowing also what popular expectation demanded of Messiah, yet living always with His face set towards Calvary, must have seen in the Cross the direct Divine alternative to the eagerly awaited Messianic war.

(2) Secondly, we are told that Pacifists forget that the Cross is *ethically not for our imitation.* "Jesus, in His death on the Cross, is not in the New Testament held up chiefly as an example for our imitation, but as the object of our faith. We are not chiefly called upon to imitate Him, but to trust Him as Saviour."[2] That is to say, Jesus, who discriminated

[1] Gal. ii. 20; v. 24.   [2] Isaac Jolly, op. cit., p. 18.

so carefully in the occasion for His own sacrifice, left
no example or rule to be followed blindly or without
discrimination. Again this is in so large a measure
true, and yet such a dangerous half-truth.
Paradoxical surely, that our critics should be so
ready for us to imitate the transcendent God in His
cosmic "wrath", and so loath that we should
imitate the Cross of God incarnate in the Man Jesus!
There is a sense in which, none would deny, Jesus'
redemptive sacrifice once for all for the world's sin
need not and cannot be repeated. Yet, whatever
be true of the New Testament as a whole, Jesus
Himself *does* hold up the Cross for His disciples'
imitation. There is no word of Jesus more often
repeated in the Gospels than that in which He bids
them follow Him along the road of the Cross.[1] Even
if He was speaking only in metaphor, He could not
have done so had He not seen in the way of life He
set before them something in common with His own
supreme sacrifice. And such a passage as the
following shows that the early Church realized that
Jesus did so call upon His disciples to follow Him:
"For hereunto were ye called: because Christ also
suffered for you, leaving you an example, that ye
should follow his steps. . . . who his own self
bare our sins in his body upon the tree."[2]

This particular objection to the Pacifist position
is perhaps due to a wrong idea of what "imitation
of the Cross" implies. The Pacifist is sometimes
accused of regarding the Cross as a mechanical
device whose efficacy depends on the power of self-
sacrifice *per se*, and then of arrogantly presuming to
"imitate the Cross" under the misconception that
any such isolated and indiscriminate act of self-
sacrifice will have a similar automatic redemptive

[1] Matt. x. 38; xvi. 24; Mark viii. 34; x. 31; Luke ix. 23;
xiv. 27.
[2] 1 Pet. ii. 21 f.

power. But the Christian Pacifist position is exactly
the reverse. Always it is not suffering as such that
redeems, but the readiness to accept suffering rather
than deny the Truth, obedience to a particular way
of life with self-sacrifice, if necessary, as a possible
climax. For Jesus the Cross meant risking everything on His conviction that God's way of overcoming evil would work. Therefore we see in the
Cross, not a mechanical act of self-sacrifice which
Jesus imagined would be effective *ex opere operato*,
but the inevitable climax, under the conditions which
confronted Him, to a consistent life-practice of
meeting evil not by violence, not even by invoking
law, but by the way of forgiving and reconciling love.
Jesus died rather than betray that love method.
So in our own problem: if there are circumstances
in which there seems no alternative to self-sacrifice,
it is precisely because any other alternative would
be a betrayal of the specifically Christian method of
overcoming evil by redemptive love. By "imitating
the Cross" we mean, not presumption in martyrdom,
but loyalty to the life-practice of redemptive love
with its possible climax in a cross, that is to say a
way of life which as a last resort is willing to sacrifice
itself rather than betray itself.

So in our international problem. A nation,
following the way of Christ, might feel called upon
to adopt a policy of total disarmament. But it
would do so, in the first instance, not with the
deliberate purpose of courting martyrdom, but with
the conviction that the best safety from the perils
against which nations arm is to be found in a new
national way of life, which would remove causes of
provocation and lead progressively to reconciliation
and peace. It, too, would risk everything on the
conviction that God's way would work. But such
a nation must also be willing, if necessary, to incur
the risk of national martyrdom by refusing to equip

itself against the possibility of aggression. And it may be that the world must wait for its redemption from warfare until one nation is ready to risk crucifixion at the hands of its possible enemies. It might lose its own national life; but it would set free such a flood of spiritual life as would save the world. To many of us this may not be a very welcome or comforting implication to discover in the Cross. Yet it may be well to remind ourselves that no interpretation of the Cross is likely to be a true one which is not to-day, as of old, an "offence" to the "Jew", and to all who like him are obsessed with "law" and "righteousness", and "folly" to the politically minded "Greek". The Pacifist interpretation of the Cross is certainly both. It may once again prove to be "the power of God, and the wisdom of God".[1]

(3) Lastly Pacifists are accused of unjustifiably narrowing the idea of "redemption", and appropriating the word "redemptive" to their own peculiar way of life. May it not be possible, we are asked, in a war waged on behalf of righteousness, for the soldier himself to become the embodiment of redemptive sacrifice, facing as he does at the call of duty and for love of a cause suffering, mutilation and death? And is there not a certain arrogance in claiming the title "redemptive", as if it were applicable only to the love which refuses to take part in warfare, because it believes that it knows a more excellent way, and refusing it to the love which lays down life on the battlefield in conflict with evil militant, because it chooses the highest way it knows and believes that love has nothing more to give? "Greater love hath no man than this, that a man lay down his life for his friends."[2] This is a fair question and must be frankly faced. Let it

[1] I Cor. i. 23.
[2] John xv. 13.

be sadly confessed that spiritual pride is apt to be
the besetting temptation, if not the besetting sin,
of Pacifists. And let it be humbly and gratefully
acknowledged that such self-sacrifice on the battlefield for pure and unselfish ends may be the symbol
of a love than which no man has a greater; let us
even admit that in a broad sense it may be
"redemptive". But it is clearly not "redemptive"
in the particular sense in which we have been using
the word. For we have been discussing two
alternative methods or lines of action for the meeting
and overcoming of evil; by "redemptive" we mean
"possessing the power to win over the will from evil
to good"; and the word has been used throughout
our discussion in the more specific sense of
"redemptive" of that particular evil against which
action is being directed, in this case what we have
just called "evil militant" in the person of my
enemy. Now let me assume (*per impossibile*, it is to
be feared) that my cause in battle is wholly right
and my enemy's wholly wrong. Even so, will my
self-sacrifice in opposition to him on the battlefield
have any "redemptive" effect on the evil aggressive
will of the enemy whom I am fighting? Possibly
yes, if my main purpose on the battlefield was to
"lay down my life" as a challenge to and protect
against aggressive wickedness. However fantastic
may be the idea of a "peace army" deliberately
sacrificing itself between the lines, it is quite possible
that its sacrifice might have some such moral effect
on the spirit of aggression. But the soldier's main
purpose in going into battle is not "to lay down his
life for his friends". If while on active service he
showed the slightest trace of such a desire for simple
martyrdom, he would promptly be disciplined. He
may be heroically willing to lay down his life; but
his main purpose, the reason for which he has been
enlisted, trained, sent to the front, is to win victory,

and to do so by killing and wounding as many of the
enemy as possible. It is not pleasant to have to
make such statements, but the subject is far too
serious to admit of any sentimentality. Now what
I have to ask is whether *that* line of action on my
part—not laying down my own life, but seeking to
take his—can possibly have any "redemptive"
efficacy, in the sense already defined, with respect to
the particular evil against which it is directed, that
is to say, the enemy I am seeking to kill. Even
supposing that I am wholly right, and he is wholly
wrong, can I possibly expect to "redeem" my
enemy, win over his will from evil to good, by doing
my utmost to kill him? It needs little knowledge
of psychology to suggest that the result is certain to
be the very opposite. And, however glorious the
by-products of war in duty and courage and self-
sacrifice, as realists we know that the soldier is on
the battlefield to kill. It would seem that the
apologist for war must be much more explicit in his
definitions, when he claims to find, even in the
by-products of such activity, something which is
"redemptive" in the same sense as is the Cross of
Jesus Christ.

Our study has seemed to prove that an essential
element in the "Gospel" of Jesus Christ is that
distinctive method of meeting and overcoming evil,
which He set forth in His teaching and illustrated
supremely in the Cross. By His words, His life,
His death, He demonstrated the power of active and,
if need be, sacrificial love to conquer evil, vindicate
the moral order, and redeem the will from evil to
good. In a word, He overcame evil with good. It
is impossible to see how one can eliminate this from
the Gospel without changing its whole character, or
exempt the Christian from a like obligation without
dismissing him forthwith from discipleship. The
principle that one cannot cast out devils by the

prince of devils is not a matter of opinion to be proved or disproved by cleverly manipulating texts: it lies at the very heart of the Christian ethic as proclaimed and lived by Jesus Christ Himself. He knew no other way of overcoming evil than by redeeming the evil will. Nor will the Christian willingly employ any methods which are not ultimately redemptive. And here surely we have the canon by which we are to judge whether this or that particular use of force can be brought within the orbit of the Christian ethic, the test by failure to pass which war is seen to be under a final prohibition. It comes under the ban mainly for two reasons: firstly, because there is in war as such no single element which is truly redemptive; and secondly, because it results in a complete prostitution of those personal values, and a complete rupture of those personal relationships, apart from which both the Fatherhood of God and the Brotherhood of man are reduced to a mere mockery. It is on this ground of the violation of human personality more than on any other ground that the Christian ethic must renounce war.

Perhaps we may state the case thus: Reconciliation and redemption, which are the supreme ends of the Christian love which is itself the essence of Christian living, can never be achieved by force pure and simple; for force in itself is much more likely to thwart than to fulfil these ends. If then force is to find a place within the Christian ethic, it must only be in a form which is limited by such sympathetic discrimination that it may be expected to prepare the way for the final appeal of redemptive love. Any use of force, therefore, which by its very nature escapes from such control, and renders such an appeal abortive, can under no circumstances be countenanced. It is obvious that war utterly fails to pass this test, and for these reasons: Firstly, no sooner has war begun than there automatically follows the prostitution of every conceivable moral value, truth, honesty, decency, upon which all stable personal relationships, and the only possibility of recovering them when lost, depend. Secondly, war has, particularly in its modern form, become so entirely mechanical and impersonal that one can engage in it only by totally depersonalizing one's entire relationship to the object of one's action.[1] And thirdly, its main aim is to kill, and therefore to remove the presumed object of redemption entirely from that sphere of personal relationship wherein alone love can make its appeal. "War, in short, of necessity, and in its essential idea, is a use of force which, from the angle of the demands of love, is a hideous cul-de-sac in personal relations"[2]—a cul-de-sac surely up which no Christian can venture to go.

[1] Attempts are sometimes made actually to defend modern warfare on the ground that it has become so impersonal: there need be no personal hatred of foe for foe; each is a machine destroying an unseen enemy, and often not even knowing whether he does so. Yet personality is the watchword of Christian theology; and right personal relationship is the key to Christian ethics. A true understanding of the mind of Jesus would suggest that there can be few actions more un-Christlike than thus to depersonalize one's attitude to one's brother man. "War represents an anti-personalistic force which regards human personalities as so much cannon fodder, as material to be used for developing the power of the State. There was after all something personal in the idea of the warlike knight—it involved personal valour. Modern war is completely devoid of this element. Armaments and preparations for war, which serve to undermine the very states which adopt these means for the sake of greater power and emancipation, constitute precisely the forces which depersonalize and dehumanize man. This state of things is quite intolerable to the Christian conscience." (Nicolas Berdyaev, in *Reconciliation*, August, 1936, p. 207.)

[2] H. H. Farmer, in *The Christian and War*, p. 6. See this pamphlet, published by The Church of Scotland Ministers' Peace Society, for an admirable treatment of this particular aspect of the subject.

VII

CHRIST AND CAESAR

WE have already remarked that neither the teaching of Jesus Himself nor the New Testament as a whole throws very much direct light upon the duty of the Christian citizen towards the State of which he is a member; and we have touched on one of the chief reasons for this fact.[1] One is inclined to regret this silence all the more because it appears inevitable that the claims of Christianity and of the State, of God and of Caesar, should constantly be coming into conflict, and this for several reasons. Christianity, whose end and goal is the Kingdom of God, has its eyes fixed and its affection set upon things unseen and eternal: the State is inevitable concerned with worldly power and temporal ends. Christianity is a universal religion, knowing no national preference: the State in practice serves exclusively the interests of its own people. Christianity, as the life of the spirit, has its vital breath in freedom: the State has always found it necessary to find its ultimate sanction in coercion and force. Christianity ascribes to human personality an absolute value and independence of all that is of the earth. The State by its claim to ultimate loyalty is compelled to deny this priority and supremacy of the personal. "For the ancients a man was primarily a citizen of his State, first a member of a community and only afterwards a personality. If Christianity has done anything new for political science and jurisprudence, it has been to reverse this order."[2] To-day we are watching the

[1] See above, p. 60.
[2] Scholten, quoted by Heering, op. cit. p. 172.

pendulum swinging once again in the opposite direction.

Hence the dilemma of the Christian Pacifist. He may be first a Christian, but he is also one of the units which compose the State. Can he accept the privileges, and at the same time contract out of the obligations, which are due to his membership of the group? Must not the individual conscience be subordinate to the common judgment? For example, when the State goes to war, must not the citizen, whatever his convictions as a Christian, acquiesce and co-operate? Must not personal responsibility be merged in civic solidarity? The Christian citizen is confronted by the sorest conflict of loyalties. "As the history both of Christendom and of Christians shows, the adjustment of the claims of these conflicting interests is a matter of the most acute difficulty. A freedom of conscience which shall escape moral anarchy, an obedience to State authority which stops short of acquiescence in evil, represent an ideal hard to define or sustain."[1]

The tension has become still more acute with the growth of the "Totalitarian State", which has thus been admirably defined by J. H. Oldham: "The totalitarian state is a state which lays claim to man in the totality of his being; which declares its own authority to be the source of all authority; which refuses to recognize the independence in their own sphere of religion, culture, education and the family; which seeks to impose on all its citizens a particular philosophy of life; and which sets out to create by means of all the agencies of public information and education a particular type of man in accordance with its own understanding of the meaning and end of man's existence." As Mussolini himself has put it: "Fascism conceives of the State as an absolute, in comparison with which all individuals and groups

[1] C. E. Raven, *Is War Obsolete?* p. 65.

are relative, only to be conceived of in their relation
to the State. . . . Nothing against the State;
nothing outside the State; everything for the
State." Now it is clear that a State which advances
such claims is in fact declaring itself to be also a
substitute for an authoritarian Church, and is
advancing a view of life which is to be accepted, if
not as an actual substitute for religion, then at least
as its powerful rival. "Underlying the claims of the
Totalitarian State are certain ultimate beliefs regarding the nature and destiny of man. In so far as
these are incompatible with the Christian understanding of the meaning and purpose of man's
existence, the Church must inevitably be involved
in a life and death struggle for its existence. . . .
It is clear that between the view that the racial and
national soul is the ultimate measure of all values,
and the view that all souls, individual and national,
are judged by the Gospel, there is an irreconcilable
conflict."[1] Nor need we delude ourselves into
believing that the danger is confined to countries
under authoritarian rule. It is present also in
Democratic States so far as such States are swayed by
the doctrine of the sovereign authority of the State,
a doctrine which really puts the State in the position
of God, with complete control over the lives and
liberties of its subjects, which it may use as it thinks
fit for its own purely selfish and national ends.
And there are few if any States which are not so
swayed. When the threat is perfectly obvious, as
in Germany to-day, the only answer may be martyrdom, and through martyrdom comes a new life.
The danger is much more subtle when Christian
people are unaware that their principles are being
undermined by the gradual paganizing of the mind
of the whole community. The new absolutism of the
State is a warning signal of dangers which confront

[1] See J. H. Oldham, *Church, Community and State*, pp. 9–12.

the whole Christian Church. For it is diametrically opposed to the basic principle of the Christian ethic, namely the sovereignty of human personality. "Above all else our epoch stands in desperate need of learning to prize man more highly, of acknowledging the value of every man, even of the least, because every single man bears within himself the image and likeness of God. For this reason one can never regard man as a means to an end, or turn him into a tool in the hands of the State, so as to aid its expansion, or encourage its desire for national self-glorification. Such at least is the Christian point of view. For Christianity man stands far higher than the State and is far more precious than the State: he is unique, an unrepeatable personality."[1]

Before we turn to the New Testament for light on our main question, "To what extent may the New Testament ethic be held to govern the Church and the individual Christian in the matter of their duty to the State?" two preliminary questions suggest themselves, which can here be merely stated rather than argued in full:

Firstly, what is the nature of the State? Are we to think of it as an arbitrary supra-moral power, whose end is always self-protection and self-aggrandisement at the expense of a supposed external "enemy"? Or shall we not rather think of it, not as an entity separate from and superior to the individual citizens of which it consists, but as a community of free individuals united by an active sense of belonging together? Shall we not hold that the essence of the State consists in its embodiment of a common purpose, this purpose being not the execution of its arbitrary will, but the preservation of law and justice as between free individuals? And will not this imply, not that the State itself creates the authority of law, but that the authority

[1] Nicolas Berdyaev, in *Reconciliation*, August, 1936, p. 207.

of the State itself depends upon the justice whose instrument it is, while this justice, from the very beginning, derives its only authority from conscience? A State, therefore, which violates the conscience of its citizens is undermining its own authority and the primary ground of its existence.

Secondly, what is the nature of the Church? Is it merely a voluntary association for religious purposes, with the right to define and from time to time readjust its standards of value and principles of action, and capable like other such voluntary associations of placing itself in the hands of the State to be used by the State for its own ends? Or is it not rather a Divine society, constituted not by the will or beliefs of men but by God Himself, the mystical Body of Jesus Christ,[1] built on the Incarnation and deriving its life and authority from supernatural sources, and as an extension of the Incarnation entrusted with the supreme task of continuing the redemptive work of Jesus Christ in the world? I have already said that all the ultimate problems of Pacifism are theological, and I must confess that many of the arguments we have to meet seem to me to be based upon a complete misapprehension of the nature of Christianity as a redemptive religion, and of the mission of the Church as the instrument of that religion in the world.

G. J. Heering has suggested that one of the chief reasons for the failure of historical Christianity to uphold the full Christian ethic in the face of a State which still claims the right to enlist the support of the Church for war is "the suppression of primitive Christian values and the false exegesis of the New Testament concurrent with it".[2] An examination

[1] See especially Eph. v. 23-32.
[2] Heering, The Fall of Christianity, p. 218. I am particularly indebted to this book for much in this chapter.

H

of our problem in the light both of the New Testament passages and of its treatment down the Christian centuries will show just how true this statement is.

Turning then, first to Scripture, we find that the claims of the State are in the main based on two New Testament passages:

Firstly there is Jesus' famous answer to the question whether or no He considered it to be lawful to pay tribute to Caesar: "Render unto Caesar the things that are Caesar's, and unto God the things that are God's."[1] This saying is not seldom used as if it meant that according to Jesus the Christian must not allow religious scruples to interfere with his duty to the State. Such a misplacing of the whole emphasis of Jesus' words is possible only if we completely ignore the context. It is worth reminding ourselves:

(a) The "Caesar" in question is not the government which a patriotic Jew would recognize as having the right to claim his allegiance. He is the representative of a foreign State holding down a conquered people by force of arms. If the saying may be used at all to sanction an unconditional claim by the State upon its subjects, then the duty indicated is not that of taking arms in defence of the State's freedom, but the duty of submission to an undesired dictatorship.

(b) The whole point of Jesus' answer is that it enabled Him to escape the trap prepared for Him by the Pharisees, who wished to force Him either to damage His reputation in the eyes of His own people by advocating submission to Rome, or to compromise Himself with the government by advocating resistance. According to ancient ideas Caesar's "image and superscription" on a coin indicated that

[1] Mark xii. 17.

it was his own property. Well, then, says Jesus, it is surely fair enough to give back to Caesar what is already his own: but see that you likewise pay your debts to God. So far from providing us with a proof-text in support of war, the words are really a Pacifist's disavowal of the policy of violent resistance to an oppressor.

(c) The words have sometimes been turned into an actual apology for war. Thus Augustine, who was one of the first Christian theologians to try to harmonize war with the New Testament, comments: "For indeed tribute is brought with the very object of giving wages to the soldiers, who are indispensable, just because of the wars."[1] But, quite apart from the fact that there is no reference either explicit or implicit to war, the impression left by the passage as a whole is that all the emphasis falls on the second clause, "and render to God the things that are God's". An excellent comment is that of the well-known French scholar Loisy (again no Pacifist): "Jesus emphasizes the lawfulness of political power and of tribute much less than the insignificance of these things in comparison with the Kingdom of heaven. . . . Let the things of this world be esteemed according to the smallness of their value, and let these duties be discharged as there is necessity; but let men know above all that the greatest things lie elsewhere, in fidelity to the heavenly Father. It would be to falsify the thought of Jesus to suppose that the debt to Caesar is on the same plane, or that it has the same absolute and definite character, as the duty towards God."[2] At most Jesus suggests that civil obedience need not necessarily clash with the obedience due to God, provided that the claims of the State do not invade the sphere of duty owed to God.

[1] *Contra Faustum*, xxii. 74.
[2] Loisy, *Les Evangiles Synoptiques*, Vol. II, p. 336.

(d) Even such a partial gesture of acquiescence in the claims of the State loses much of its force when we remember that Jesus' view of the Kingdom of God implied that the rule of Rome was doomed to destruction, and that it would be overthrown not by man's agency but by God's. Why then quibble over so small a matter as the payment of taxes? The head of Caesar on the coin stamps it as his own. Well, then, give him his own, for the time being. But the matter of real importance is your loyalty to God!

But the crowning proof-text of a militarist theology, and the basis of the whole traditional dogma concerning the relation of Church to State, has always been Paul's apology for the "higher powers", which must be quoted in full: "Let every soul be in subjection to the higher powers: for there is no power but of God; and the powers that be are ordained of God. Therefore he that resisteth the power, withstandeth the ordinance of God: and they that withstand shall receive to themselves judgment. For rulers are not a terror to the good work, but to the evil. And wouldst thou have no fear of the power? do that which is good, and thou shalt have praise from the same: for he is a minister of God to thee for good. But if thou do that which is evil, be afraid; for he beareth not the sword in vain: for he is a minister of God, an avenger for wrath to him that doeth evil. Wherefore ye must needs be in subjection, not only because of the wrath, but also for conscience sake. For for this cause ye pay tribute also; for they are ministers of God's service, attending continually upon this very thing. Render to all their dues: tribute to whom tribute is due; custom to whom custom; fear to whom fear; honour to whom honour."[1] We make the following observations:

[1] Rom. xiii. 1-7.

(a) It seems not unlikely that Paul is here echoing the words of Jesus which we have just been discussing, and the passage must be read in the light of those words. For Paul is always to be interpreted by reference to Jesus, not Jesus by reference to Paul. It may be willingly conceded that Paul, who had himself experienced the benefits of Roman civil protection and seems to have been more than a little susceptible to the glamour of the imperial idea,[1] puts a much greater stress than did Jesus on the duty of civil obedience. When we remember how he invoked the protection of Roman law, used the great military roads, relied for security and ease of travel upon the Pax Romana, it is little wonder that he saw in Roman law and order a divinely ordained instrument to assist the cause of His Master. Paul realized, too, the need of effecting a working understanding between Christianity and the civil authority,[2] and saw that this implied on the part of Christians a willingness to make certain concessions to the powers that be: they are to be loyal so far as such loyalty does not violate the higher loyalty due to Christ. It is interesting, however, to speculate whether Paul would have written in quite the same terms of the Roman "powers" if this letter had been penned at the close of his own life, still more if he had already seen the beginnings of a general persecution of the Church. The Book of Revelation itself shows the revulsion of feeling of which the Christian Church was capable.

(b) When we base an argument on such words as "there is no power but of God; and the powers

[1] He boasts of his Roman citizenship (Acts xxii. 28); he saw in Rome's discipline the force which prevented the final breaking in of the power of anti-Christ (2 Thess. ii. 7); he turns Rome's political system into spiritual metaphors (Phil. iii. 20); the goal of his missionary efforts is the Imperial City herself (Acts xix. 21; xxiii. 11).

[2] Similarly this appears to have been one of the motives of the author of the Book of Acts.

that be are ordained of God",[1] it is important to be quite clear, first about Paul's meaning, and second about what we are trying to prove on the basis of that meaning. Does Paul mean that the principle of ordered government for the protection of justice is divinely ordained? Or does he mean that any particular government, which happens to be in power, is so because God Himself has ordained it? Clearly the former is the basic truth underlying his words. Yet it is perfectly obvious that the Apostle, believing as he does that on the whole the Roman government is a power for good, writes the words with the particular government of the day in view.[2] But when basing an argument upon Paul's words it is necessary for us to distinguish between the ideal State, as we have defined it above,[3] that is to say the body of citizens in their corporate capacity as the guardian of law and liberty, and the particular Government which happens to be in control at any given time. Such an ideal State we may well admit to be "ordained of God". But to insist upon a perfectly literal acceptance of the surface-meaning of Paul's words is to prove far too much. Not only would the existence of an ordered and authoritative civil government be proved to be "ordained of God", but any gang which might set itself up as "the higher powers", and presumably any policy however godless, would likewise be declared to be "of God". Taking into consideration the circumstances under which Paul writes, and his desire that the infant Church should so far as possible keep on good terms with the civil authority, it is clear that these words of the Apostle must be used with no less

[1] Rom. xiii. 1.
[2] We feel the same difficulty with reference to the words which the Fourth Evangelist puts on Jesus' lips before Pilate: "Thou wouldest have no power against me, except it were given thee from above."—John xix. 11.
[3] P. 112 f.

careful discrimination than his much less tactful
sayings about women and marriage. Yet traditional
theology has again and again used the words to
support the State's claim to unconditional authority
over the will of its subjects.

(c) The use commonly made of the words "he
beareth not the sword in vain"[1] likewise results in
proving far too much. The Apostle, it is argued,
is here asserting that "the power" has an absolute
and presumptive right to use what force he thinks fit
(amounting if necessary to war) for the resistance of
evil and the furtherance of State interests. But
Paul was writing to the Christians at Rome, whose
"higher powers", then no less than to-day, had no
thought of limiting the use of force to what would
now be considered moral ends. Our opponents
cannot have it both ways. They may not claim the
support of this text for an anti-pacifist position, and
then go on to explain that of course Paul, no less
than they themselves, was thinking of the kind of
force which a modern "Christian" government
would employ. If the words sanction the use of
force at all, then it is the kind of force with which
Paul's readers were familiar, a use of force which
included wars of aggression, the enslavement of
captives, the martyring of Christians. Which again
suggests that it is well to temper our interpretation
of Paul by reference both to Jesus' own teaching and
also to the peculiar circumstances under which the
Apostle was writing.

(d) In any case there is no explicit reference here
to war: it is very doubtful whether it is even
implicit; probably the question of war never
entered Paul's mind as he wrote these verses. The
issue before him is the attitude of the "power" to
the good and the bad citizen. Clearly then the
"power", as even the wording of the Westminster

[1] Rom. xiii. 4.

Confession implies, is the "civil magistrate", and the "sword" is the symbol of the "civil authority". No more may be deduced from the passage than the right of the civil authority to maintain order with a police force, which will restrain the evil-doer and bring him before a responsible judge. The ethical distinction between such measures and the indiscriminate and irresponsible violence used in war, whereby the sword becomes an "avenger for wrath" not only to "him that doeth evil" but to the helpless and the innocent, is basic to any sane pacifist position. If it be objected that what is to-day the duty of a police-force was in the Roman world a military function, the reply is that the converse holds good also: it would be just as true to say that, so far as Paul himself had experience of it, the function of the military in the Roman world was the maintenance of civil order. It was thus that Paul knew the Roman soldier, and would doubtless approve of him. In the same way not a few Pacifists, the author included, would approve of an "International Police Force", even of soldiers, if it was operating in a virtually disarmed world. The "soldier" would then be a "policeman" in fact and not merely in name.

(e) The whole passage must then be read as Paul's apology, written under the special circumstances which we have tried to indicate, for a system of civil government, which he admits indeed to be of Divine appointment, but would hardly allow to lie within the order of grace as revealed by Christ. Such a Christian order of society rests upon a different and higher principle, which is concisely stated in the very next paragraph[1]; this may be summarized in its concluding words: "Love worketh no ill to his neighbour: love therefore is the fulfilment of the law." It is only in the light of what follows that we

[1] Rom. xiii. 8–10.

can see these verses, which we have just been
discussing, in their true perspective.

(f) It is very important also to recognize the close
connection of the section with the great pacifist
paragraph, ending with the watchword, "Be not
overcome of evil, but overcome evil with good,"
by which it is immediately preceded.[1] Some of the
older commentaries note this connection and explain
it thus: the preceding " pacifist " verses have
suggested to Paul that he should next go on to
safeguard the Christian Ethic, as intended by him
to apply in the sphere of individual conduct, against
possible misapplication in the sphere of civil
obligation. "The idea of the civil power may have
been suggested by verse 19 of the preceding chapter,
'Avenge not yourselves', etc., as being one of the
ministers of the Divine wrath and retribution;
. . . at any rate the juxtaposition of the two
passages would serve to remind St. Paul's readers
that the condemnation of individual vengeance and
retaliation does not apply to the action of the State
in enforcing law; for the State is God's minister,
and it is the just wrath of God which is acting
through it."[2]

But it is hardly in the manner of the Apostle,
first to expound the very essence of the ethic of
Jesus, as he does in xii. 9–21, and then to proceed
to qualify it. It is therefore not surprising that our
most modern English Commentary on *Romans* treats
the present passage, not as a qualification of the way
of life laid down in the previous chapter, but as an
illustration of its application. Thus Professor C. H.
Dodd,[3] after quoting the words, "Be not overcome
of evil, but overcome evil with good," as "the most

[1] Rom. xii. 17–21.

[2] Sanday and Headlam, *Romans*, in I.C.C., p. 366.

[3] See *Romans*, in the *Moffatt New Testament Commentary*,
pp. 202–4.

creative element in Christian ethics", goes on to show how in the present passage Paul picks out the relation of the Christian to the State as one of the spheres within which he may practise that ethic. The famous words in Romans xiii. are in fact intended to urge upon the Church that same Pacifist attitude to the State which was adopted by Jesus Himself. Incipient hostility on the part of the State is to be met not with resistance but with the submissiveness of those who know that "to them that love God all things work together for good".[1] "We can hardly doubt that the possibility existed that the Church might by committed by Jewish-Christian enthusiasts to a disastrous policy of opposition to the Government." The verses in question are therefore "to be read, in the first instance, as a definite repudiation, on behalf of the Church, of the Zealot tendency in Judaism, which was already gathering strength for the final outbreak, and might well have repercussions among Christians. Paul makes his statement quite absolute. Yet he was clearly prepared to disobey in the case of a conflict of loyalties. But he is thinking of contumacious defiance of the Empire such as was advocated by Jewish fanatics. Upon those who rebel, the legal penalty of rebellion will fall; and this, he seems to imply, is in fact the Divine judgment on their action. It is tempting to see here a reference to the saying attributed to Jesus in Matthew xxvi. 52: 'Put up again thy sword into its place; for all they that take the sword shall perish by the sword.'" We see, therefore, that these verses, which have too often been used to buttress the State's alleged divinely ordained authority to demand the citizen's service in war, might be much more aptly used to prove that Jesus' pacifist outlook was shared to the full by His great Apostle.

[1] Rom. viii. 28.

(g) It is now possible to see how the passage fits in with what was said above[1] concerning the "Wrath" of God. The traditional translation of verse 4, "he is a minister of God, an avenger for wrath to him that doeth evil", is somewhat misleading. The magistrate is rather "a divine agent bringing the penalty of Wrath upon the evil-doer". "We then get Paul's theory of civil government in its true setting. It is part of the natural moral order, or divine appointment, but lying outside the order of grace revealed in Christ. It exhibits the principle of retribution just as it is exhibited in the natural laws of cause and effect to which the body and mind of man are subject. . . . The retributive system of justice in a non-Christian society is also a manifestation of the same principle. . . . The Christian takes no part in the administration of a retributive system; but, in so far as it serves moral ends, he must submit to it."[2]

A study of the earliest Christian interpreters of Scripture shows without any ambiguity the relative value which they placed upon the claims of Caesar and the claims of God. They all echo the Apostles' cry, "We must obey God rather than men."[3] Admittedly, after the end of the second century the evidence of the Christian Fathers is much less unambiguous. The problem is further complicated by the fact that service in the army would involve, not only the violation of a pacifist ethic, but also an oath of loyalty to the Emperor and participation in heathen religious rites. The latter, rather than any objection to war as such, is commonly stated by non-pacifist apologists to be the chief reason for the refusal of Christians to take part in war. The question is much too involved to be treated fully

[1] Pp. 75 ff.
[2] Dodd, *Romans*, p. 204.
[3] Acts v. 29.

here.[1] But the following two statements may be made with some assurance:

Firstly, until about the close of the third quarter of the second century the attitude of the Church was quite consistently Pacifist. Harnack's conclusion is that no Christian would become a soldier after Baptism at least up to the time of Marcus Aurelius, say about A.D. 170.[2] After that time signs of compromise become increasingly evident, but the Pacifist witness continues strong right up into the fourth century. Aristeides, Justin Martyr, Tatian in the second century, Tertullian, Origen, Cyprian, Hippolytus in the third, Lactantius in the fourth, all make statements which show that they regard war as organized sin and a denial of the way of Jesus. In the Canons of Hippolytus it is stated that a soldier who confesses himself a Christian convert is to be excluded from the sacrament until he has done penance for the blood which he has shed.

Secondly, whatever influence the fear of pagan contamination may have had, when these writers give their reason for denouncing military service, it is nearly always the straight Christian-Pacifist objection which is stated; war is the antithesis of Christianity: "The weapons of blood are discarded, that the weapons of peace may be girded on." As Harnack again admits, and there is no greater authority on the age in question, the chief reason for the offence which the military profession gave to the earliest Christians was that "it was a war-calling, and Christianity had absolutely renounced war and the shedding of blood". Here are some characteristic statements; note how again and again the antithesis between Christian discipleship and the soldier's calling is underlined:

[1] See C. J. Cadoux, *The Early Church and the World*, for an adequate discussion.
[2] Harnack, *Militia Christi*, p. 47 f.

Justin Martyr (c. 150) declares that, while Christians will gladly die for Christ's sake, "We refrain from making war on our enemies. . . . For Caesar's soldiers possess nothing which they can lose more precious than their life, while our love goes out to that eternal life which God will give us by His might."[1] Clement of Alexandria, though elsewhere he shows traces of ambiguity, says (c. 200) that Christ "with His word and with His blood gathers the army that sheds no blood". "We Christians", writes Origen (first half of third century) "no longer take up sword against nation, nor do we learn to make war any more, having become children of peace, for the sake of Jesus who is our leader." "As we by our prayers vanquish all demons who stir up war . . . we in this way are much more helpful to the kings than those who go into the field for them. . . . And none fight better for the king than we do. We do not indeed fight under him, although he require it, but we fight on his behalf, forming a special army, an army of piety, by offering our prayers to God."[2] "Shall it be held lawful", asks Tertullian (a. 200), "to make an occupation of the sword, when the Lord proclaims that he who uses the sword shall perish by the sword? And shall the son of peace take part in battle when it does not become him even to sue at law?"[3] "How shall a Christian man wage war, nay, how shall he even be a soldier in peace-time, without the sword, which the Lord had taken away? For although soldiers had come to John, and had received the formula of their rule; although even a centurion had believed; the Lord afterwards, in disarming Peter, ungirded every soldier."[4] Cyprian (died 258)

[1] *Apology*, I, II, 39.
[2] *Contra Celsum*, v. 33; viii. 73.
[3] *De Corona*, xi.
[4] *De Idololatria*, xix.

protests against the dual standard of morality which brings it about that "if a murder is committed privately it is a crime, but if it happens with State authority courage is the name for it".[1] And as late as the beginning of the fourth century we find Lactantius declaring: "It will not be lawful for a just man to serve as a soldier, for justice itself is his military service, nor to accuse anyone of a capital offence because it makes no difference whether thou kill with a sword or with a word, since killing itself is forbidden. And so, in this commandment of God, no exception at all ought to be made to the rule that it is always wrong to kill a man, whom God had wished to be regarded as a sacrosanct creature."[2] These statements will appear all the more striking if we remember that they are made by men for whom the Old Testament, with its frequent glorification of nationalism and militarism, was the Word of God in as full a sense as the New. "They were saved", writes Cadoux, "by the soundness of their own moral intuitions from drawing from these ancient precedents the erroneous conclusions affecting their own conduct, which some modern controversialists are so eager to draw from them."[3]

It is surprising that orthodox theology is still so blind to the witness of primitive Christianity, and remains tied hand and foot by the traditional dogma of Church and State which was laboriously evolved from the beginning of the fourth century onwards. For the crucial change in the attitude of the Church to the claims of Caesar began, of course, after the conversion of the Emperor Constantine to Christianity in 312. The Faith was now exalted, or debased, into a State religion, and Christians

[1] *Epistles*, I, 6.

[2] *Divinae Institutiones*, vi. 20, 15–17.

[3] Cadoux, *The Early Church and the World*, p. 118; quoted by Heering, op. cit. p. 47, to whom I also owe several of these quotations.

naturally began to look to the State for patronage, and in return more and more become reconciled to Caesar's claims, even where these might seem to compromise the New Testament ethic. And, as usual, war provides the touch-stone. The result of this changed attitude is thus summarized by Harnack: "After the winning over of Constantine the barrier between the *milites Christi* and the army was removed. The *milites Christi* put themselves at the disposal of the Emperor. The soldier of Christ became *ipso facto* a soldier of Caesar."[1] The Church even went the length of pronouncing the primitive Christian attitude liable to punishment, and as early as 314 the Council of Arles decreed that "they who throw away their weapons in time of peace shall be excommunicated". Harnack rightly terms this decision "astonishing and shocking", and adds that by it "the Church completely revised her attitude to the army and war; . . . She even created saints on behalf of the Christian soldiers, and relegated to the monastic orders her old views about war".[2]

It was Athanasius, "the Father of orthodoxy", who was one of the first to set the seal of official approval upon a subservience to State claims which involves in fact a double-morality; and once again it is the question of war which provides the test: "Murder is not permitted", he writes, "but to kill one's adversary in war is both lawful and praiseworthy."[3] Augustine, too, vigorously defends the right of the State to require the service of Christians in war, which for him always appears as a police measure against evil-doers. One can almost hear the modern dictator's apology for a "civilizing" war of aggression: "He who is bereft of his freedom,

[1] *Militia Christi*, p. 87.
[2] Op. cit. p. 92.
[3] Athanasius: *Epistle to Ammonius*.

because he misused it by doing evil, is conquered in his own best interests."[1]   Yet Augustine is quite obviously troubled in conscience by the dual ethic which his hypothesis involves; and in his great work *De Civitate Dei* he is the first systematically to define the relations between the Church and the State.   He insists that the *Civitas Terrena*, as represented by the Roman Empire, is both ordained of God and under God's sovereignty, and that God righteously uses it as an instrument of war for the accomplishment of His will: "So likewise does He with the times and ends of war, be it His pleasure justly to correct or mercifully to pity mankind, ending them sooner or later, as He wills."[2]   Yet he cannot wholly break with the older antithesis between Church and State, for according to him it is only in the *Civitas Dei*, which he practically identifies with the Church, that God's reign is perfectly manifested and the Christian ethic can come to its full expression.

Obviously such a wavering attempt to harmonize conflicting loyalties could not permanently satisfy the demands of a Catholic theology which was becoming more and more subservient to the State. The dualism between Church and State, so apparent in Augustine's *Civitas Terrena* and *Civitas Dei*, is resolved into a systematic unity by Thomas Aquinas (thirteenth century), who insists far more strongly than Augustine, not only that the political State exists in the providence of God, but also that it is the natural and indispensable foundation of the Kingdom of Grace as represented by the Church. State and Church together thus become a single *corpus Christianum*.   The Church might have "conquered" the world, but in at least an equal measure the world had penetrated the Church, and

[1] *Epistle to Marcellinus*, xiv.
[2] *De Civ. Dei*, v, 22.

the purity of the Christian ethic suffered correspond-ingly. Aquinas is still the Catholic apologist *par excellence* for the "just war", when it is "waged by the command of the ruler for a righteous cause and with a good intention".[1] But Catholicism after Aquinas was driven to recognize that the keenest Christian consciences were certain still to feel the tension between the earthly citizenship and the citizenship of the Kingdom of God. It therefore more and more encouraged such to withdraw from the world into the cloister, where alone pure Christian truth might be lived out. Of course this is, in fact, a recognition of a dual Christian standard: and it is still the Roman Catholic solution of the insoluble question, how to preserve both a Christianity which is subservient to a non-Christian or semi-Christian State and also the full Gospel ethic.

The development of Reformed thought is even more significant. Luther, in his revolt against the cloister, was obliged to insist that the pure ethic of the Sermon on the Mount was the true life for every Christian. When compelled to come to some understanding with the State, he still retained the idea of a single *corpus Christianum*; but he took refuge in the explanation that this "body" con-sisted of two "domains" a spiritual and a worldly; the one, in which the Christian is under the sanctify-ing grace of God, the other "put under the sword", in which by the ordinance of God evil men are kept in restraint and outward peace and order preserved by the State. These two domains demand a different

[1] In view of a recent utterance of the Archbishop of Canterbury it is worth noting that the expression "*just* war", so often used by Apologists both Catholic and Protestant, is a translation of the Latin, where "*justum* bellum" means, not a war ethically "righteous", but a "*regular*" war sanctioned by the Govern-ment, as opposed to private feuds or brigandage. In the original sense of the phrase Mussolini's Abyssinian adventure was a "just war"!

I

morality; for the "order of grace" there is a personal
morality based on the Sermon on the Mount; for
the "order of creation" there is a State morality;
and only the former is wholly Christian. When we
ask, as we are bound to ask, how the Christian who
has to live in both these domains can contrive thus
to practise a dual morality, Luther replies that in his
personal life and relations he must abide by the first
order and the full ethic of the Gospel: as a Christian
citizen he must abide in loyalty to the second order
which is "put under the sword". "In spirit
Christians are subject to none but Christ alone, but
with life and goods they are nevertheless subject to
the secular authority, and obliged to be obedient
to it."[1] The antithesis accordingly is now not
between two distinct classes of people, as in the
Catholic solution; the two conflicting types of ethic
are, as Troeltsch puts it, "brought together into a
dual way of life for every individual; the compromise is shifted to more deeply inward ground".[2]
Luther frankly draws the conclusion that, whatever
be true of the inward personal life, the entire outward life of the Christian is to be in submission to
the sovereign and to the sovereign's conceptions of
the will of God. And once again the implications of
such a doctrine come out most clearly with respect
to war: "The hand which bears such a sword (the
sword of government) is as such no longer man's
hand but God's; and not man it is, but God, who
hangs, breaks on the wheel, beheads, strangles and
wages war. . . . It is not I that smites, thrusts
and kills, but God and my Prince, whose servants are
my hand and life."[3] When Luther's teaching is thus
set forth, it is difficult perhaps to realize that this

[1] *Ob Kriegsleute auch in seligem Stande sein können*, Luthers
Werke; Weimar Ed., XIX, p. 629.
[2] *Die Soziallehren der Christlichen Kirchen und Gruppen*,
p. 505; quoted by Heering, op. cit. p. 75.
[3] *Ob Kriegsleute*, p. 626.

doctrine is still the orthodox basis in the Protestant world for the dominant view concerning the ethics of Church and State. Yet it can hardly be called a solution of the problem at all; for man is one personality, and possesses one inward and spiritual life, which, so far from being exclusive of his outward life, is deeply affected by it, and in turn very largely determines it. As Troeltsch justly remarks: "The Protestant way out of the strain of a dual morality, personal and official, is not a solution, but a reformulation of the problem."[1]

It must be confessed that Calvin comes no nearer than does Luther to an adequate solution. While taking over many of Luther's arguments he thinks to avoid the dualistic character of Lutheran ethics, and the discrepancy between personal and State morality, by insisting that God's Word comes to a man in Scripture as a whole, that this Word when related to human conduct comes primarily as a commandment, and that therefore even in the Old Testament commandments, one and all, we are to recognize, not a relatively Christian ethic, but one that is wholly Christian. The obvious contradiction between the thorough-going love-ethic of the Sermon on the Mount and the savage demands of Old Testament nationalism is resolved as follows: God's love is primarily the love of the Sovereign, who by His omnipotence elects some and reprobates others; similarly man's love is above all else the will to give God the glory that is His due by keeping His commandments, as they are laid down in Old Testament and New Testament alike. Calvin can thus see the *corpus Christianum* as a single, undivided "domain". "God's glory is involved in this alliance of Church and State. And everything that can minister to that glory is not only permitted but required, and does not need the expedient of a

[1] Op cit. p. 509.

so-called 'official morality' to justify it."[1]   In
particular Calvin has no difficulty in justifying war;
for he can always appeal to the Old Testament, with
which the Sermon on the Mount, in view of the unity
of Scripture, cannot be in conflict. As Heering
remarks at the close of an interesting study,
"Calvinism has thus solved the problem of
Christianity and State morality by bringing the
State and its instruments of power under a
'Christian' law, basing this law mainly on the Old
Testament, and putting the New Testament motive
of love in the background".[2] When it is objected
that the New Testament nowhere gives its sanction
to war, but rather condemns it outright, Calvin
replies that war is a concern of the State, that the
causes which the Old Testament heroes found for
waging war still remain, and that "in this respect
Christ altered nothing whatever by His coming".

It is as well that we should frankly recognize that
it is upon this foundation of bad theology and worse
Scriptural interpretation that the teaching of the
Westminster Confession is based, when it declares in
Chapter XXIII, "God, the supreme Lord and King
of all the world, hath ordained civil magistrates to
be under Him over the people for His own glory and
the public good; and, to this end, hath armed them
with the power of the sword, for the defence and
encouragement of them that are good, and for the
punishment of evil-doers. . . . *Christians* . . .
*may lawfully, now under the New Testament, wage war
upon just and necessary occasions*."[3] If war be, as
we believe we have demonstrated, contrary to the
ethic of the Gospel, then so long as the Christian
citizen assents to the State's claim to wage a "just
and necessary" war, just so long is he also assenting
to the doctrine of a dual-ethic and a radical

---

[1] Heering, op cit. p. 82.   [2] Op. cit. p. 82.
[3] Cf. also the 37th Article of the Church of England.

distinction between personal and collective morality. The Church has largely lost the moral leadership of the world because it has taken this road of compromise, and to-day even in Christian circles this countenancing, often no doubt almost unconsciously, of such a double standard of morality is playing havoc with the sincerity of our entire Christianity. What is to be the final outcome? "If Christianity does not set itself against this exalting of the State above morality, the spirit of the world will soon enough break loose from its fastness of non-moral political power, and will gradually re-conquer every region which the Christian conscience has subdued to itself in the course of twenty centuries."[1]

It is certain that the tension between the ethics of Church and State, between Christ and Caesar, can never wholly be resolved. For both occupy a common field of action on which neither can afford to give way. The Church, no less than the State, is committed to the belief that the life of man finds its meaning and fulfilment only in a community of persons, free persons, but still units in a community. And only in relation to such a community can the Church fulfil her mission. "It is no longer sufficient that the Church should bear its witness only or chiefly to individuals. Its witness can be effective only as a continual challenge and criticism of the prevailing ideas and ways of life, in so far as these are contradictory of the Christian understanding of man and his responsibilities. In a community consciously committed to a contrary view, and most of all where the State has adopted a totalitarian policy, this witness can be borne only at the cost of suffering and martyrdom."[2] Our problem inevitably resolves itself into the question as to where our final

---

[1] Max Huber, *Internationale politiek en Evangelie*, p. 26; quoted by Heering, op. cit. p. 166.
[2] J. H. Oldham, *Church, Community and State*, p. 19.

loyalty lies; and the conflict of loyalties can be resolved only in the old way: "We must obey God rather than men."[1] The Christian Pacifist does not deny that the State is a Divine institution; he only affirms that there are certain State activities which the Christian conscience can never endorse. He gives due loyalty to Caesar, but he also recognizes that a point is sometimes reached when a choice must be made between defiance of Caesar and apostasy from Christ. He is willing to render to Caesar the things that are Caesar's, but only when he is not thereby precluded from rendering to God the things that are God's.

[1] Acts v. 29.

VIII

WHAT ABOUT IT?

IT may not be amiss to repeat at this point that our primary concern here is not with the practical issues, and that it is no part of our purpose to argue that the way of Jesus Christ, as we have seen it set forth in the New Testament, offers the world an easy way out of its difficulties. If it did it would not be the way of the Cross. Nor shall we discuss at any length whether or no a Pacifist policy is a wise or even a practicable policy for our country to-day; this has been done often and admirably elsewhere.[1] To thoughtful Christians nothing surely can be more disturbing than the fact that, when the Church discusses war and peace, the questions which usually arise are not on fundamentals—such as our conception of God and His purpose for the world, the authority of Christ and the scope of His Kingdom, the nature of the Church and her redemptive mission, the Christian conception of personality and the Christian method of overcoming evil—but on matters of political expediency, special instances and probable consequences: "What would happen if . . .?" "What should we do when . . .?" God as an active factor in the situation seems too often to be entirely left out. This book has been written in the conviction that the Christian Church has no right even to ask such questions, until she has first satisfied her conscience that she sees clearly what is the mind of Jesus Christ and whither His way leads. When she has done so she will follow

[1] See especially the pamphlet by Aldous Huxley. *What are you going to do about it? The Case for Constructive Peace.*

that way, without undue concern that the world counts it quixotic, and in the faith that an act of obedience might well be answered by an outpouring of Divine Power which would change the whole world situation in ways we cannot even dream. If this be deemed incredible, what is there left for faith to cling to? Can we then in a few simple propositions sum up, in the light of our study of the New Testament, the duty of the Christian and of the Church?

(1) Firstly, whatever be the verdict concerning the practicability of the way of Jesus under modern conditions, the Church will once again frankly confess, as she did at the first, that both His teaching and His practice are unequivocally "pacifist", in the sense in which the word has been used throughout our study, and can lend no sanction whatever to war, which is rather seen to be the supreme denial of all that He taught and everything for which He stood. Christian Pacifism is admittedly a position which bristles with notorious difficulties, and one can respect the candour of those who say: "All this is sentimental moralizing; the New Testament ethic is impracticable and impossible; the simple truth is that Jesus was wrong; we are living in London or Rome or Paris or Berlin, not in the Kingdom of Heaven or a Fool's Paradise." Such a position is at least unambiguous, even though we may believe that it is grievously mistaken and that Jesus will prove to be the true Realist after all. One need not dwell on the possibly disastrous consequences of following Jesus' way in order to see the certain disaster which had already resulted from rejecting it. One also has a certain sympathy with the man who refuses to water down the challenge of the Gospels, but has come to the conclusion, though with a painful sense of guilt and frustration, that for the time being and in a world such as this we must rest content with the

second-best. But it is difficult to have any respect
for the kind of apologetic which brings down Christ's
standards to the level of our own poor attainments,
and seeks to comfort the uneasy conscience by
suggesting that really He meant no more than a
well-meaning Genevan politician. The out-and-out
neo-pagan militarist at least realizes that a nation
cannot serve both Christ and Mars. "The Christian
faith", writes General Ludendorff, "and the life
shaped by it, are the prime causes of a national
breakdown in the totalitarian war."[1] Yet some
Christians still think to make Mars respectable by
decking him out in a Gospel uniform.

(2) Secondly, we shall insist that for the Christian
the question of participation in war is ultimately a
personal issue. The problem of war is morally so
serious just because for so many it has become a
matter of conscience. And there is only one kind
of conscience, the individual conscience. Every
ethical movement gets its power from the attitude
of persons, and all collective convictions draw their
moral worth from the consciences of individuals.
It becomes more and more clear that there are
certain policies which a certain kind of State will not
abandon, unless it is coerced into doing so by the
moral resistance of the Christian Church. But this
moral resistance of the Church will never take shape
and become effective, unless Christian individuals,
even when still a minority among their fellow Church
members, offer a resolute example by an act of
personal decision. Therefore, war as a moral
problem is not merely a national or State concern,
but is primarily a personal concern. The assumption that the moral "duty" of a Christian citizen
can be scheduled for him by the State strikes at the
very roots of moral responsibility. For, as is

[1] *The Nation at War*, by General Ludendorff. Translation by
Dr. A. S. Rappoport.

admitted in all realms outside the military, "duty"
is a compulsion to be accepted from within, not to
be imposed from without. Nor is it possible, as is
so often argued, for the State to relieve the individual
of his own moral responsibility. This, for example,
is the argument of Schleiermacher when he says:
"It is clear that the subject lays no guilt on himself
if he takes up arms at the State's behest." He may
register his protest in the name of conscience, but
having done so unavailingly he is then "free from
all responsibility", for he acts "simply as a subject",
who "like all subjects obeys the behest of the
government".[1] One replies that eternal values are
to be found in God and the human soul alone. It is
the individual man who sins or is given grace, who
is to be judged and either acquitted or condemned;
and no single moral responsibility can be lifted from
his own shoulders and placed upon the State, as upon
some intermediary being between himself and God.
So long as he assents to that which his conscience
declares to be capable of no moral sanction, he is
personally responsible for sinning against the light
he has. Schleiermacher retorts that when a man
thus obeys his own conscience "conscientiousness is
losing its sense of proportion. To exclude oneself
from participating in war because it does not seem
just is sheer revolution." Not the first time that
Christian disciples have been charged with "turning
the world upside down!"[2] Nor perhaps could there
be any better treatment for the topsy-turvy world
in which we live!

(3) Thirdly, in view of our study of the New
Testament teaching concerning Church and State,
the Christian will refuse to recognize the legitimacy
of a dual standard of morality, one ethic for the

---

[1] Schleiermacher, *Die Christliche Sitte*, p. 284, quoted by
Heering, op. cit. p. 260.
[2] Acts xvii. 6.

Christian *qua* Christian, another for the Christian citizen when acting as a unit in the State. We shall insist that for the Christian there can be only one ethical standard, that of Christ's teaching, and only one morality, that which results from contact with Christ and with the Spirit of His Gospel. The Christian cannot admit that the State is in any way sacrosanct, or endowed with any divinely-ordained supra-moral authority which gives it the right to ride rough-shod over the conscience of the individual Christian citizen. No doubt the nations to-day are only so far Christian that the political morality of a "Christian" nation will be based at best on a certain compromise. But not every compromise can be accepted by the Christian citizen. Where the Christian ethic has been reduced to zero point, and all Christian values have been sacrificed to political expediency or "hard necessity", he will feel that the limit of compromise has been long overpassed. And so it is with war; for we cannot be too clear about this, that the modern war-mentality is utterly heedless of morality, provided only that the desired end be attained. Hence a Christian public opinion is slowly but surely forming which unconditionally rejects war, as we have come to know it to-day, as incapable of any moral sanction. The argument that modern war is less defensible ethically than war in the past is commonly rejected as purely sentimental. Yet one must admit the cogency of the truth, expressed by Hegel in his *Logik*, that all things have their measure and that, when the measure is passed through quantitative alteration, there is a qualitative change also: "things cease to be what they were." There is surely some moral obtuseness about the man who can see no ethical difference between, let us say, the defence of Thermopylae by Leonidas and his Spartans, and the next "defensive war", about which Mr. Stanley Baldwin has said, "There is no power on earth that can protect you from being bombed; whatever people tell you, the bomber will always get through. . . . The only defence is offence, which means that you have to kill women and children more quickly than the enemy if you want to save yourselves." Heering has admirably expressed the reason for this growing conviction among Christians that, whatever be said of past wars, war in the future can never be morally justified: "We ascribe the change to the crossing of two lines of development: that of Christian humanitarianism, and that of the practice of war. The one rising, the other sinking, have met and crossed, in the minds of thousands, whether they are conscious of it or not, like the diagonals of a square. The point of intersection marks the limit of the morally admissible and tolerable; the limit is reached and already far overstepped. Wherefore they cannot recognize war any more, whatever, its goal. They must condemn it without any qualification, in every circumstance."[1]

(4) The Church will acknowledge anew that, in distinction from the nation in its secular capacity, she has a peculiar function which can be fulfilled only when she commits herself unreservedly to the way of Christ as she sees it, without undue consideration of what appears to be immediately prudent or expedient. When she is asked, "What would happen if in the event of invasion Great Britain went pacifist?" "What practical suggestions have you for solving the present international tangle?" she will certainly try to give reasons for the faith that is hers; but she will also reply that it is no concern of hers to produce, like a rabbit out of a conjurer's hat, a way of escape from an impasse which has resulted from the nation's blind trust in policies which for twenty years she has consistently

[1] Op. cit. p. 201.

denounced as un-Christian, and certain to lead to another Armageddon. What is her concern is to set her face uncompromisingly against these policies as wholly inconsistent with Christian faith and practice, to seek to bring in some new reconciling factor by an honest attempt to apply Christ's principles, and to count the world well lost if only she can break the vicious circle, and save humanity from being brought in another twenty years to a similar impasse. When the House of Commons has itself declared[1] that "this House affirms its belief in the futility of War" and "views with grave concern the worldwide preparations for war", it is surely not too much to expect that the Church will proclaim unequivocally the Christian alternative, rather than continue to qualify her Gospel, so that it may still be fitted into an economy of armed force which has admittedly brought civilization to the edge of the abyss. It has been evident for some time that the Church can no longer preserve her self-respect merely by dotting the "i's" and crossing the "t's" of our more idealistic politicians. The Church should be in advance of public opinion, not merely echo it; she will rightly forfeit her right to moral leadership if she leaves to free-lance politicians and economists the championship of what is implicit in her own Gospel. To-day the Disarmament Conference is ignominously dead; the League of Nations has completely failed to put any check upon another mad race in armaments; during the recent Abyssinian tragedy the League Powers showed a masterly inactivity in the matter of putting into effect those measures for curbing an aggressor which they have time and again declared to be necessary unless the Covenant is to be betrayed. In view of all this it is surely high time that the Church reconsidered her position, and seriously put her mind to her alternative contribution

[1] February 5th, 1936.

to the cause of peace. Until she does so her critics may be excused for doubting whether she still believes that she has an alternative policy. She has always taught that the way of Christ is certain to be victorious over evil, if only men are prepared to make the necessary sacrifice and commit themselves entirely to it. Either she still believes this, or else she must be done with pious platitudes, and must acknowledge that Christianity is not the conquering power it has been preached to be, but must confine its programme and its ideals within the limits set by a self-centred nationalism.

(5) As a first step in this new lead the Church will refuse to countenance war under any circumstances whatever, partly because even such a bare act of renunciation will signify a clean cut with the policy which has led to the present "Fall of Christianity", but chiefly because such a refusal is a necessary clearing of the way for a positive policy of reconciliation which must otherwise inevitably be stultified from the outset. She will state explicitly that the basis of her war-refusal is her reading of the mind of Jesus Christ; not that she will decline to co-operate with all who are fighting war for any reason born of a genuine hatred of it; but the Church's distinctive contribution must be specially moral and religious, to proclaim war as essentially hateful to God and the supreme denial of the mind and the method of Christ. Moreover, she will announce to the world that her refusal to countenance war is absolute. To the objection that the essence of Christian living is not to bind oneself in advance, but to seek to read the will of God in each new situation as it arises, she will reply that every new situation grows out of a previous one, and that to fail to break with past policies is to share the guilt of creating a "new situation" in which the way of Christ will be no less "impracticable" than it is declared to be to-day.

Merely to proclaim that war is in general un-Christian, but that circumstances alter cases, is to invite the reply, which will be buttressed by all the forces of an unscrupulous propaganda, that the special circumstances have arrived and general principles must go by the board. Nothing short of an absolute refusal, solemnly affirmed in advance of the crisis and before passions have been aroused, will serve. There can be little question that if all Christians were to announce that henceforth they would have nothing whatever to do with the war method; if the Church as such were to give notice that under no conditions would she give her official blessing to war measures; and if this pronouncement were made on a definitely religious basis, so that governments might know that no amount of propaganda would move millions of their best citizens to break a vow made before God, the whole world situation would be radically changed. The ideal, of course, is united action by the Church in all nations; failing that, one national Church must take the initiative; until it does so, individual Christians must continue to bear unremitting witness. After all, is not that the story of almost all the great redemptive movements of mankind?

(6) Next, the decks having thus been cleared, the Church will be free, as to-day she is not, to take the lead in advocating such national policies as will remove the causes from which war is apt to arise. The British Government's tentative offer to confer with other Governments as to how the Empire's natural resources might be made more accessible to the unsatisfied needs of all nations, is but one indication of the kind of positive contribution to peace, involving it may be national surrenders and sacrifices, which a rich and powerful Empire should be ready to make, if her aim is not merely to maintain a privileged *status quo*; but to establish peace

founded on justice. But all this, it is to be feared, implies a radical change of heart on the part of the whole nation. In virtue of the extent of her territory and population, her political status and prestige, her unrivalled command of economic and financial resources, the British Empire is in a quite unique position for initiating a new movement towards a Christian international order based on justice and equality and a readiness for mutual sacrifice for the common good. Yet how unprepared the nation is to seize this opportunity is clear enough when even a statesman so honoured for his idealism as Anthony Eden can declare on behalf of the Government: "Nobody should imagine that because we, in Great Britain, wish passionately for peace, that fact presents an opportunity for inducing us to abandon direct and vital British interests as the price of peace. To conceive this would be gravely to misunderstand British character and temperament."[1] That such an attitude, which would be severely criticized in a private individual, should in a politician be praised as the height of patriotism, is proof enough of the extent to which even Christians have reconciled themselves to a dual standard of morality. If there is to be a national change of heart, then the Church must point the way.

(7) Though the Christian cannot in his own person acknowledge one type of ethic *qua* Christian and another type of ethic *qua* citizen, yet he may concede that the witness, to which as a Christian he knows himself to be called, cannot reasonably be expected of a State which is still in large measure sub-Christian. It must be frankly recognized that the obligation and ability fully to practise the Christian ethic is strictly relative to the status of discipleship. The Church's own duty, as the organ of Christ's redemptive purpose, is one thing: the extent to

[1] Mr. Eden, as reported in the Press, July 20th, 1936.

which her principles can be operative in a community which does not accept her presuppositions, is quite another. There are, no doubt, those who can conscientiously say, "The highest good for me is my country." They will therefore subordinate all else to their highest good, and if they imagine, even mistakenly, that war can ever advance that good, then they will conscientiously serve their country in war. The Christian, however, knows a higher good, a realm of eternal values, the Kingdom of God. And that Kingdom is otherwise served. Yet we ought to admit that it is reasonable enough for a sub-Christian State sometimes to see no better way than war whereby it can register its moral recoil against the onslaught of aggressive evil. For those who have not accepted the Christian way such a position has a large measure of validity. Only those have a right to be Pacifists who see and are committed to that interpretation of the way of Jesus. For others duty may for the present quite conceivably lie along other lines. If a man has not seized the significance of the Cross as the only true Christian reaction to evil, then it is better for him to react by the way of war than not to react at all. War in such a case may be relatively right for that man, though he will be the first to admit that he is but choosing the lesser of two evils. But it is impossible to believe that God will ever face the wholly consecrated Christian with a dilemma in which there is only a choice of two evils. As Leyton Richards has put it, "No Christian need be caught in such a dilemma; for there is always an exit from a choice of evils by the way of the Cross or its equivalent, if only men have sufficient faith to take it. . . . Jesus believed that in the struggle with moral evil the way of the Cross was more potent than the way of the sword; and His followers therefore are justified in finding a similar escape from their

K

dilemmas."[1] The Christian will never freely and personally participate in any methods of meeting evil which he does not believe to be ultimately redemptive, while at the same time he will realize that this is a prohibition laid upon his conscience by presuppositions which others do not accept. This raises the very important and difficult question how far a Christian may give a qualified approval to the employment by the State of methods of meeting evil (e.g. "sanctions", an "international police force") which he believes to be sub-Christian, and yet recognizes as a step in the right direction and the best protest against evil which can be expected of a sub-Christian community; and how far, as a Christian, he has at the same time the right to refuse personally to participate in such measures—not because he does not regard a second-best policy as at least better than a policy of *laissez-faire*, but because he feels called to a higher witness, and for him to take active part in the second-best makes impossible the prosecution of the best. Is, or is this not, equivalent to countenancing a dual standard of morality? Personally we would agree with C. E. Raven: "For myself, at least, it seems plain that along with the insistence upon the highest and a constant protest on behalf of perfectionism, we must be content to recognize a step by step development, and to excuse, *in others though not in ourselves*, the inevitable concessions which we make when we accept the best possible under the circumstances."[2]

(8) Finally, the Church's witness against war will be only, so to speak, a bringing to a focus of a wider witness against everything in our social and economic way of life which inevitably produces conflict, not only between nations, but within the nations themselves. If at the moment we have isolated war for

[1] *The Christian's Alternative to War*, p. 86 f.
[2] *Is War Obsolete ?* p. 108.

special consideration, it is on the ground that a great moral problem is often best tackled at its most acute angle. But he who is committed to the Christian Pacifist faith quickly discovers that he is committed to more than perhaps he at first realized. As one prominent Pacifist has admirably put it: "There is something shockingly inconsistent in the man who grows indignant about international war, yet is content to grow rich out of the present industrial system, to see its disputes settled by force, open or disguised, and generally to live by a scale of values which is entirely acquiescent in its tangled and ruptured personal relationships. Pacifism which is not part of a transvaluation of all values, a sacrificing witness over the whole breadth of our living, can hardly rebut the charge of sentimentalism which is so often laid against it." Above all we Pacifists must learn to face the possible cost of peace. The man who in his own soul's life has experienced the miracle of reconciliation finds that a new obligation has been laid upon him. Himself reconciled to God through the sacrificial love of Jesus Christ, he knows himself to be called to serve that same holy love, and to follow that same reconciling way in all his dealings with his fellow-men, and to do so even when the way of obedience seems likely to be the way of appalling risk and sacrifice. It led Jesus to the Cross. But beyond the Cross was the Resurrection; and it was Jesus Crucified and Risen who, when "the disciples were assembled in fear, . . . stood in the midst and said unto them, Peace be unto you."[1]

[1] John xx. 19.

APPENDIX

THE NEW TESTAMENT SPEAKS

THE ROOTS OF WAR

"Whence come wars and whence come fightings among you? Come they not hence, even of your pleasures that war in your members? Ye lust, and have not: ye kill, and covet, and cannot obtain: ye fight and war; ye have not because ye ask not." (James iv. 1 f.)

"The works of the flesh are manifest, which are these . . . enmities, strife, jealousies, wraths, factions, divisions . . . of the which I forewarn you, . . . that they which practise such things shall not inherit the kingdom of God. But the fruit of the Spirit is . . . peace. . . . Against such there is no law." (Gal. v. 19–23.)

"Ye cannot serve God and mammon." (Matt. vi. 24.)

THE WAY OF PEACE

"Glory to God in the highest, and on earth peace among men of good-will." (Luke ii. 14.)

"Peace I leave with you; my peace I give unto you: not as the world giveth give I unto you." (John xiv. 27.)

"Blessed are the peacemakers: for they shall be called sons of God." (Matt. v. 9.)

"The fruit of righteousness is sown in peace for them that make peace." (Jas. iii. 18.)

"How beautiful are the feet of them that preach the gospel of peace." (Rom. x. 15.)

"Stand therefore . . . having shod your feet with the preparation of the gospel of peace." (Eph. vi. 14 f.)

"I therefore, the prisoner in the Lord, beseech you to walk worthily of the calling wherewith ye were called, with all lowliness and meekness, with longsuffering, forbearing one another in love; giving diligence to keep the unity of the Spirit in the bond of peace." (Eph. iv. 1-3.)

"Follow after peace with all men, and the sanctification without which no man shall see the Lord." (Heb. xii. 14.)

"The God of peace shall bruise Satan under your feet shortly." (Rom. xvi. 20.)

"Finally, brethren . . . be perfected; be comforted; be of the same mind; live in peace: and the God of love and peace shall be with you." (2 Cor. xiii. 11.)

"The peace of God, which passeth all understanding, shall guard your hearts and your thoughts in Christ Jesus." (Phil. iv. 7.)

THE VICTORY OF SELFLESSNESS

"Take my yoke upon you and learn of me; for I am meek and lowly in heart: and ye shall find rest unto your souls." (Matt. xi. 29.)

"Have this mind in you, which was also in Christ Jesus: who, existing in the form of God, counted not the being on an equality with God a thing to be grasped, but emptied himself, taking the form of a servant. . . . He humbled himself, becoming obedient even unto death, yea, the death of the cross. Wherefore also God highly exalted him, and gave unto him the name which is above every name; that in the name of Jesus every knee should bow." (Phil. ii. 5-10.)

"Blessed are the poor in spirit: for theirs is the kingdom of heaven. Blessed are the meek: for they shall inherit the earth." (Matt. v. 3, 5.)

"Ye know that the rulers of the Gentiles lord it over them, and their great ones exercise authority over them. Not so shall it be among you: but whosoever would become great among you shall be your minister; and whosoever would be first among you shall be your servant: even as the Son of man came not to be ministered unto, but to minister, and to give his life a ransom for many." (Matt. xx. 25-8.)

"Whosoever shall exalt himself shall be humbled; and whosoever shall humble himself shall be exalted." (Matt. xxiii. 12.)

"God resisteth the proud, but giveth grace to the humble. Humble yourselves therefore under the mighty hand of God, that he may exalt you in due time." (1 Pet. v. 5 f.)

THE COMMANDMENT OF LOVE

"Thou shalt love the Lord thy God with all thy heart, and with all thy soul, and with all thy mind. This is the great and first commandment. And a second like unto it is this, Thou shalt love thy neighbour as thyself. On these two commandments the whole law hangeth." (Matt. xxii. 37–40.)

"The whole law is fulfilled in one word, even in this; Thou shalt love thy neighbour as thyself." (Gal. v. 14.)

"Love worketh no ill to his neighbour: love therefore is the fulfilment of the law. . . . Owe no man anything, save to love one another." (Rom. xiii. 10, 8.)

"Love your enemies, and pray for them that persecute you; that ye may be sons of your Father which is in heaven." (Matt. v. 44 f.)

"A new commandment I give unto you, that ye love one another; even as I have loved you, that ye also love one another. By this shall all men know that ye are my disciples." (John xiii. 34 f.)

"If a man say, I love God, and hateth his brother, he is a liar: for he that loveth not his brother whom he hath seen, cannot love God whom he hath not seen." (1 John iv. 20.)

"Love suffereth long, and is kind; love . . . seeketh not its own, is not provoked, taketh not account of evil; . . . beareth all things, believeth all things, hopeth all things, endureth all things. Love never faileth." (1 Cor. xiii. 4 ff.)

"The Lord make you to increase and abound in love toward one another, and toward all men." (1 Thess. iii. 12.)

"Seeing ye have purified your souls in your obedience to the truth unto unfeigned love of the brethren, love one another from the heart fervently." (1 Pet. i. 22.)

"Above all things be fervent in your love among yourselves; for love covereth a multitude of sins." (1. Pet iv. 8.)

THE DUTY OF FORGIVENESS

"Jesus said, Father forgive them; for they know not what they do." (Luke xxiii. 34.)

"Whensoever ye stand praying, forgive, if ye have aught against any one; that your Father also which is in heaven may forgive you your trespasses." (Mark xi. 25.)

"If thy brother sin, rebuke him; and if he repent, forgive him. And if he sin against thee seven times in the day, and seven times turn again to thee saying, I repent; thou shalt forgive him." (Luke xvii. 3 f.)

"Put on therefore . . . a heart of compassion . . . forbearing one another, and forgiving each other, if any man have a complaint against any; even as the Lord forgave you, so also do ye." (Col. iii. 12 f.)

"Let all bitterness, and wrath, and anger, and clamour, and railing, be put away from you, with all malice: and be ye kind one to another, tenderhearted, forgiving each other, even as God also in Christ forgave you." (Eph. iv. 31 f.)

CHRIST'S WAY OF MEETING EVIL

"Christ also suffered for you, leaving you an example, that ye should follow his steps: who did no sin, neither was guile found in his mouth: who, when he was reviled, reviled not again; when he suffered threatened not; but committed himself to him that judgeth righteously." (1 Pet. ii. 21 ff.)

"I came not to judge the world, but to save the world." (John xii. 47.)

"When his disciples saw this, they said, Lord, wilt thou that we bid fire to come down from heaven, and consume them? But he turned and rebuked them." (Luke ix. 54 f.)

"Being reviled, we bless; being persecuted, we endure; being defamed, we intreat." (I Cor. iv, 12.)

"One only is the lawgiver and judge, even he who is able to save and to destroy: but who art thou that judgest thy neighbour?" (Jas. iv. 12.)

"All things therefore whatsoever ye would that men should do unto you, even so do ye also unto them." (Matt. vii. 12.)

"Love your enemies, do good to them that hate you, bless them that curse you, pray for them that despitefully use you." (Luke vi. 27 f.)

"Resist not him that is evil: but whosoever smiteth thee on thy right cheek, turn to him the other also." (Matt. v. 39.)

"Why not rather take wrong? Why not rather be defrauded?" (I Cor. vi. 7.)

"The Lord's servant must not strive, but be gentle towards all . . . forbearing in meekness, correcting them that oppose themselves." (2 Tim. ii. 24.)

"Bless them that persecute you; bless, and curse not. . . . Render to no man evil for evil. . . . If it be possible, as much as in you lieth, be at peace with all men. Avenge not yourselves, beloved, but give place unto wrath: for it is written, Vengeance belongeth unto me; I will recompense, saith the Lord. But if thine enemy hunger, feed him; if he thirst, give him to drink: for in so doing thou shalt heap coals of fire upon his head. Be not overcome of evil, but overcome evil with good." (Rom. xii. 14 ff.)

"See that none render unto any one evil for evil; but alway follow after that which is good, one toward another, and toward all." (I Thess. v. 15.)

"Finally, be ye all likeminded, compassionate, loving as brethren, tenderhearted, humbleminded: not rendering evil for evil, or reviling for reviling; but contrariwise blessing; for hereunto were ye called, that ye should inherit a blessing." (I Pet. iii. 8 f.)

THE WAY OF THE CROSS

"God commendeth his own love towards us, in that, while we were yet sinners, Christ died for us." (Rom. v. 8.)

"Jesus the author and perfecter of our faith, who for the joy that was set before him endured the cross, despising shame." (Heb. xii. 2.)

"Forasmuch then as Christ suffered in the flesh, arm ye yourselves also with the same mind." (1 Pet. iv. 1.)

"We are pressed on every side, yet not straitened; perplexed, yet not unto despair; pursued, yet not forsaken; smitten down, yet not destroyed; always bearing about in the body the dying of Jesus, that the life also of Jesus may be manifested in our body." (2 Cor. iv. 8–10.)

"If any man would come after me, let him deny himself and take up his cross, and follow me." (Matt. xvi. 24.)

"Wherefore Jesus also, that he might sanctify the people through his own blood, suffered without the gate. Let us therefore go forth unto him without the camp, bearing his reproach." (Heb. xiii. 12 f.)

THE MINISTRY OF RECONCILIATION

"If, while we were enemies, we were reconciled to God through the death of his Son, much more, being reconciled, shall we be saved by his life; and not only so, but we also rejoice in God through our Lord Jesus Christ, through whom we have now received the reconciliation." (Rom. v. 10 f.)

"It was the good pleasure of the Father that in him should all the fulness dwell; and through him to reconcile all things unto himself, having made peace through the blood of his cross." (Col. i. 19 f.)

"He is our peace, who made both one, and brake down the middle wall of partition, having abolished in his flesh the enmity . . . that he might create in himself of the twain one new man, so making peace; and might reconcile them both in one body unto God through the cross, having slain the enmity thereby: and he came and preached peace to you that were far off, and peace to them that were nigh." (Eph. ii. 14–17.)

"All things are of God, who reconciled us to himself through Christ, and gave .unto us the ministry of reconciliation; to wit, that God was in Christ reconciling the world unto himself, not reckoning unto them their trespasses, and having committed unto us the word of reconciliation." (2 Cor. v. 18 f.)

THE FAMILY OF NATIONS

"I bow my knees unto the Father, from whom every family in heaven and on earth is named." (Eph. iii. 14 f.)

"Wherefore, putting away falsehood, speak ye truth each one with his neighbour: for we are members one of another." (Eph. iv. 25.)

"In one spirit were we all baptized into one body, whether Jews or Greeks, whether bond or free; and were all made to drink of one Spirit." (1 Cor. xii. 13.)

"For there is no distinction between Jew and Greek: for the same Lord is Lord of all, and is rich unto all that call upon him." (Rom. x. 12.)

"There can be neither Jew nor Greek, there can be neither bond nor free, there can be no male or female: for ye are all one man in Christ Jesus." (Gal. iii. 28.)

"There cannot be Greek and Jew, circumcision and uncircumcision, barbarian, Scythian, bondman, freeman; but Christ is all, and in all." (Col. iii. 11.)

THE MORAL EQUIVALENT OF WAR

"Fight the good fight of faith, lay hold on the life eternal." (1 Tim. vi. 12.)

"This is the victory that hath overcome the world, even our faith." (1 John v. 4.)

"For though we walk in the flesh, we do not war according to the flesh (for the weapons of our warfare are not of the flesh, but mighty before God to the casting down of strong holds); casting down imaginations, and every high thing that is exalted against the knowledge of God, and bringing every thought into captivity to the obedience of Christ." (2 Cor. x. 3–5.)

"For our wrestling is not against flesh and blood, but against the principalities, against the powers, against the world-rulers of this darkness, against the spiritual hosts of wickedness in the heavenly places. Wherefore take up the whole armour of God, that ye may be able to withstand in the evil day, and, having done all, to stand." (Eph. vi. 12 f.)

"Take thy part in suffering hardship, as a good soldier of Christ Jesus." (2 Tim. ii. 3.)

"I have fought the good fight, I have finished the course, I have kept the faith: henceforth there is laid up for me the crown of righteousness, which the Lord, the righteous judge, shall give to me at that day: and not only to me, but also to all them that have loved his appearing." (2 Tim. iv. 7 f.).

INDEX OF SCRIPTURE PASSAGES